MW01195642

Uttermost

CONSISTING OF

PROPOSITIONS FOUR THROUGH EIGHT

FROM

THE APOLOGY FOR
THE TRUE CHRISTIAN DIVINITY

BY

ROBERT BARCLAY

EDITED BY JASON R. HENDERSON

**This and other publications
are available FREE upon request
by contacting:**

Market Street Fellowship
981 W. Market Street Akron, Ohio 44313
email: MSFPrinting@gmail.com
phone: 330-419-1527

www.marketstreetfellowship.com
© 2017 – v1

"Therefore He is also able to save to the uttermost those who come to God through Him."

—Heb. 7:25

Contents

FORWARD

Robert Barclay (1648–1690) was a Scottish Quaker, and one of the most eminent writers among the early Society of Friends. His *Apology for the True Christian Divinity* was first published in 1675, and came to be considered the definitive exposition and defense of Quaker principles for the next 200 years.

Barclay was born into opulence and educated in some of the finest schools of the time, where his natural genius gained the admiration of both teachers and peers. In addition to English, he was early a master of the Greek, Hebrew, French, and Latin languages, and so excelled in his studies that his uncle (the Rector of the Scotts College at Paris) offered to make him his heir. But at seventeen years of age, upon entering a meeting of the people called Quakers, Robert Barclay said, "I felt a secret power among them which touched my heart." And as he continued with them, he "came to receive and bear witness of the Truth," not being convinced, he said, "by strength of argument, or by a particular discussion of each doctrine, but by being secretly reached by Life. And as I gave way to it, I found the evil weakening in me and the good raised up, and so I became thus knit and united to this people, hungering more and more after the increase of the Power and Life of Christ whereby I might feel myself perfectly redeemed."

The *Apology for the True Christian Divinity* (from which this book is taken) was first written in Latin when Barclay was only 27 years old, and afterwards translated by himself into English. In the preface to the original edition we find the following remarks:

"Perhaps my method of writing may seem not only different, but even contrary, to that which is commonly used by the men called theologians, with which I am not concerned; for I confess myself to be not only no imitator and admirer of the schoolmen, but an opposer and despiser of those by whose labor I judge the Christian religion to be so far from being bettered, that it is rather destroyed. Nor have I sought to accommodate my work to itching ears, who desire to comprehend in their head the sublime notions of Truth, rather than to embrace it in their heart. For what I have written comes more from my heart than from my head; from what I have heard with the ears of my soul and seen with my inward eyes, and my hands have handled of the Word of Life. What has been inwardly manifested to me of the things of God, that do I declare; not so much minding the eloquence and excellency of speech, as desiring to demonstrate the efficacy and operation of Truth. And if I err sometimes in the former, it is no great matter; for I act not here the grammarian or the orator, but the Christian; and therefore in this I have followed the certain rule of the Divine Light, and of the Holy Scriptures. Indeed, what I have written is written not to feed the wisdom, knowledge, and vain pride of this world, but rather to starve and oppose it."

"Unto you these following propositions are offered; and if they be read and considered in the fear of the Lord, you may perceive that simple, naked truth which man, by his wisdom, has rendered so obscure and mysterious. Alas, man has burdened the world with great and voluminous treatises and commentaries, and rendered truth a hundredfold more dark and intricate than it is in itself. All of man's school learning, which takes up most of a lifetime to learn, brings not a bit nearer to God, nor makes any man less wicked or more righteous than he was. Therefore God has laid aside the wise and the learned and the disputers of this world, and has chosen a few despicable and unlearned instruments (as he did fishermen of old), to publish his pure and naked Truth, and to free it from the mists and fogs wherewith the clergy has clouded it. And among many others whom God has chosen to make known these things—seeing I also have received, in measure, grace to be a dispenser of the same Gospel—it seemed good unto me, according to my duty, to offer unto you the following propositions. Though they are short, yet they are weighty, comprehending much and declaring what the true ground of knowledge is, even that knowledge which leads to Life Eternal. To this Life I bear witness, and leave my testimony to the Light of Christ in all your consciences. Farewell."

Robert Barclay
Ury, Scotland, 25th of 9th Month, 1675

The following pages contain five of the original fifteen propositions from Barclay's *Apology*, treating upon the fall, redemption, justification, and perfection of man. Because the great majority of modern readers find the original language and style of Barclay unmanageable, and because many are unfamiliar with the theological debates and common criticisms against the Quakers at the time of his writing, I have felt it appropriate to somewhat modernize, edit, and annotate these five propositions. I understand and respect the opinion of those who oppose the editing of early Quaker writings, saying rightly that these were native English speakers, and knew well how to speak for themselves. Even so, I have found very few today who have been able or willing to wade through the original publications (a task I nevertheless highly recommend[1]), and I doubt very much that ancient Friends would have desired their style or vocabulary to be a stumbling block in the way of the modern reader. This version is not for the historian, the purist, or the theologian, but for the present day seeker of Truth, and I can say, without any misgivings, that my only aim in re-publishing Barclay is the glory of Truth and the good of immortal souls.

Jason Henderson
February 2017

---

[1]   The unabridged and unedited version of Barclay's *Apology* is available through Quaker Heritage Press. www.qhpress.org

Chapter I

The Condition of Man in the Fall

We come now to examine the state and condition of man as he stands in the fall—what his capacity and power is, and how far he is able, of himself, to advance in relation to the things of God. Truly, a thorough understanding of this subject is of great use and service, because from the ignorance and altercations that have surrounded it, there have arisen great and dangerous errors, both on the one hand and the other. Some have exalted the light of nature, or the faculties of the natural man, as being capable (by man's own will, light, and power) to follow what is good and make real progress towards heaven. Others, however, have run to the other extreme, not only confessing (rightly) that men are incapable of themselves to do good, and prone to evil; but also suggesting that infants still in their mother's womb, before committing any actual transgression, are contaminated with a true guilt whereby they deserve eternal death. Indeed, many have not been afraid to affirm that poor infants are eternally damned and must forever endure the torments hell. But the God of Truth, having now again revealed His Truth by His own Spirit, has taught us to avoid both of these extremes.

In this chapter, I therefore propose to show, first—the condition of man in the fall, and how far incapable he is in meddling with the things of God; and second—that God does not impute evil to man until he actually joins with it.

The Nature and Extent of Man's Fall

As to the first, it is not my desire to dive into the various notions and conjectures which many have asserted concerning the condition of Adam before the fall. All agree in this: that by transgression he came to a very great loss, not only in the things which related to the outward man, but in regard to that true fellowship and communion he had enjoyed with God. This loss was signified unto him in the command, "For in the day that you eat of it you shall surely die."[1] This death could not have been an outward death, or the dissolution of the outward man, for Adam's body did not die till many hundreds of years after. So the death spoken of must necessarily relate to the immediate loss of spiritual life and communion with God.

The consequence of this fall is also expressed in these words: "So He drove out the man; and He placed cherubim at the east of the Garden of Eden, and a flaming sword which turned every way, to guard the way to the tree of life."[2] Now whatever literal or outward signification this might have had, we may also safely ascribe to this paradise a spiritual meaning, and rightly understand it as that spiritual communion and fellowship which the saints obtain with God by Jesus Christ. Only to Christ do these cherubim

---

[1]   Genesis 2:17

[2]   Genesis 3:24

give way, and to as many as enter by the One who calls Himself the Door. So then, though we do not ascribe any part of Adam's *guilt* to men, until they make it theirs by similar acts of disobedience; yet we cannot believe that the descendants of Adam have any good thing in their nature, as belonging to it; for he from whom they derive their nature had nothing good in himself to pass along to them.

If then we may affirm that Adam did not retain in his nature (as belonging to it) any will or light capable of giving him knowledge or experience in spiritual things, then neither can his posterity. So then, whatsoever real good[3] any man does, proceeds not from his nature as a man, or as a son of Adam, but from the Seed of God in him, from a new visitation of life given to bring him out of this natural condition. But though this gift or Seed be *in* man, it is not *of* him, and this the Lord plainly declared; for when speaking of fallen man, He testified "that every imagination of the thoughts of his heart was only evil continually."[4] These words are very clear and comprehensive. Observe the emphasis of them: First, He says "every imagination of the thoughts of his heart;" so that this allows no exception in any thoughts of man's heart. Secondly, "is only evil continually;" it does not say 'partially evil continually,' nor 'entirely evil at some times;' but it is both *only* evil and *continually* evil! This certainly excludes any good as belonging to man's heart naturally: for that which is only evil, and always evil, cannot of its own nature produce any

---

3   Editor's Note: Not things judged to be good by the fallen, dark, and selfish perspective of the creature, but that which is truly good, as coming from the Source of goodness Himself, and aiming towards His eternal purpose.

4   Genesis 6:5

good thing. The Lord expressed the same thing again a little after, saying, "The imagination of man's heart is evil from his youth," again inferring how natural and inherent evil is to every son and daughter of Adam. So then, if man's thoughts are always and only evil, and that from his youth, it is certain and undeniable that the thoughts of man are altogether useless and ineffectual to him in the things of God.

Furthermore, this appears clearly from that saying of the prophet Jeremiah, "The heart is deceitful above all things, and desperately wicked."[5] For who can seriously imagine that a heart such as this has any power of itself, or is in any way fit, to lead a man to righteousness, seeing that its own nature is directly the opposite? This is as contrary to reason, and is as impossible in nature, as to suggest that a stone, of its own nature and ability, should fly upwards.

The apostle Paul treats the condition of men in the fall at large, taking various descriptions from the Old Testament: "There is none righteous, no not one. There is none that understands; there is none that seeks after God. They have all turned aside, they have together become unprofitable. There is none that does good, no not one. Their throat is an open tomb; with their tongues they have practiced deceit; the poison of asps is under their lips, whose mouths are full of cursing and bitterness. Their feet are swift to shed blood; destruction and misery are in their ways, and the way of peace they have not known. There is no fear of God before their eyes."[6] What more could be said? Paul seems to be particularly careful that no good be

---

[5]   Jeremiah 17:9
[6]   Romans 3:10-18

ascribed to the natural man, showing how he is polluted in all his ways, void of righteousness, understanding, and the knowledge of God, out of the right way, and entirely unprofitable. And if this be the condition of the natural man as he stands in the fall, he is most certainly unfit to take one right step toward heaven.

Objection: If it be suggested that this text of the apostle does not speak of the condition of all men in general, but only of some particulars, I answer:

Answer: The text clearly speaks to the contrary in the foregoing verse, where the apostle applies these things to himself (in his natural condition) and to all Jews and Gentiles, saying: "What then? Are we better than they? Not at all. For we have previously charged both Jews and Gentiles, that they are all under sin, as it is written:" and so he goes on, showing that he speaks of mankind in general.

Objection: If they object that the same apostle says in the foregoing chapter that the Gentiles "do by nature the things contained in the Law,"[7] and so consequently do by nature that which is good and acceptable in the sight of God, I answer:

Answer: The word "nature" here cannot be understood of man's own nature, which is corrupt and fallen, but of that spiritual nature which proceeds from the Seed of God in man as he receives a visitation of God's love and is quickened by it. This clearly appears by the following words,

---

[7]   Romans 2:14

where Paul says, "These not having the law" (i.e., the written law) "are a law unto themselves, who show the work of the law written in their hearts." Thus whatever good deeds appear are the effect of God's law written in their hearts. And seeing that Scripture plainly declares the writing of the law in the heart to be part of the New Covenant dispensation, this can be no consequence or part of man's fallen nature.

Moreover, if the "nature" here mentioned could be understood of man's own nature, then the apostle would unavoidably contradict himself, since he elsewhere positively declares, that "the natural man does not receive the things of the Spirit of God, for they are foolishness to him; nor can he know them."[8] Now I hope all will confess that the Law of God is among the things of God, especially as it is written in the heart. And the apostle, in the 7th chapter of the same epistle, says that "the Law is holy, just, and good;" and that "the Law is spiritual, but I am carnal." Now in what respect is he carnal, except as he stands unregenerate in the fall? We see then that the apostle makes a clear distinction between the Law which is spiritual, and the nature of man which is carnal and sinful. Thus, even as Christ says that "grapes cannot be expected from thorns, nor figs from thistles," so neither can the law (which is spiritual, holy, and just) be fulfilled by a nature that is corrupt, fallen, and unregenerate.

From all of this we conclude (and with good reason), that the "nature" here spoken of (Rom. 2:14) by which some Gentiles are said to have done things contained in the Law, is not the common and fallen nature of man, but

---

[8]   1 Corinthians 2:14

the spiritual nature that arises from the righteous and spiritual law written on the heart by the finger of God.

Guilt Imputed to Transgressors

I come now to discuss the other part, namely, that this evil and corrupt seed is not imputed to infants until they actually join with it. For as Paul relates in Ephesians 2, they "are by nature children of wrath, *who walk* according to the prince of the power of the air, the spirit that now works in the children of disobedience." Here the apostle gives their evil walking as the reason of their being children of wrath. And this is in keeping to the whole strain of the Gospel, where no man is ever threatened or judged for the iniquity he has not actually committed. But in the case of those who continue in iniquity, and so do approve the sins of their fathers, God will visit the iniquity of the fathers upon the children.

But alas, as has been stated, many among Protestants and Catholics are not ashamed to declare openly that infants, even in their mother's wombs, are contaminated with true guilt whereby they deserve eternal death. Now, is it not strange that men should entertain an opinion so absurd in itself, and so cruel and contrary to both God's mercy and justice, and concerning which the Scripture is altogether silent? Is it not manifest that man has invented this opinion out of self-love, and from that bitter root from which all errors do spring? For most Protestants who hold this opinion think that they and their children rest securely in the absolute decree of God's election; and since they deem themselves incapable of missing salvation, they have no great difficulty in assigning all others, both old and young, to hell. For seeing that self-love (which is always apt to believe whatever it desires) fills them with a hope that their part is secure, they are not too concerned how this may leave their neighbors, which happen to be the far greater part of mankind.

The Catholics, on the other hand, use this opinion as an artful means to increase esteem for their church, and reverence for its sacraments, seeing they pretend that Adam's guilt is only washed away by their form of infant baptism. These, perhaps, appear a little more merciful, in that they do not send unbaptized children to hell, but rather to *limbo*—concerning which concept the Scriptures are also entirely silent.

Such ideas are not only absent from Scripture, but contrary to the express tenor of it. The apostle plainly says, "Where there is no law there is no transgression,"[9] and again, "But sin is not imputed, where there is no law."[10] Now clearly to infants there can be no law, seeing they are utterly incapable of receiving and comprehending it. The law cannot reach to any but those who have, in some measure, less or more, the exercise of their understanding. But those who are under a physical impossibility of either hearing, knowing, or understanding any law—where the impossibility is not brought upon them by any act of their own, but is according to the very order of nature appointed by God—to such there is no law.

Furthermore, what can be more certain than the word of God to Ezekiel, "The soul that sins, it shall die. The son

---

9   Romans 4:15
10   Romans 5:13

shall not bear the guilt of the father, nor the father bear the guilt of the son"[11] The prophet here first shows the true cause of man's eternal death, which in his own sinning. Then, as if he purposed expressly to shut out such an opinion, he assures us, "The son shall not bear the iniquity of the father, etc." From which I thus argue: If the son does not bear the guilt of his father, or of his immediate parents, far less shall he bear the guilt of Adam.

Having thus far shown how absurd this opinion is, I shall briefly examine the reasons that some contend for it.

Objection: First, they insist that Adam was the head of a corporate race, and therefore all men sinned in him, as being still in his loins. And for this they allege Romans 5:12, where the apostle says, "Therefore, just as through one man sin entered the world, and death through sin, and thus death spread to all men, because all sinned."

Answer: To this I answer: That Adam is the head of a corporate race is not denied by us, nor that through him there is a seed of sin propagated to all men, which in its own nature is sinful, and inclines men to iniquity. Nevertheless, it does not follow from this that infants, who do not willingly join with this seed, are accounted guilty. And as for these words of Paul in his letter to the Romans, the reason for the guilt is there plainly stated, "because all sinned." But that infants cannot be counted among these guilty ones is plainly shown in the following verse: "But sin is not imputed where there is no law."

---

[11]   Ezekiel 18:20

Objection: Their second objection is from Psalm 51:5, "Behold, I was brought forth in iniquity, and in sin my mother conceived me." Hence, they say, it appears that infants are guilty even from their conception.

Answer: How they infer this conclusion, for my part, I do not see. The iniquity and sin here appear to be far more ascribable to the parents than to the child. David says, "In sin my mother conceived me;" he does not say, "My mother conceived me a sinner." But even if the sin here mentioned should be ascribed to the child, we confess freely that a seed or nature of sin is transmitted to all men from Adam, in which seed all are given occasion to sin, and this is the origin of all evil actions and thoughts in men's hearts. But, again, we insist (according to plain Scripture) that this evil is imputed or credited to none, until by actually *sinning*, they willingly join with it.

Objection: Thirdly, they object, that "the wages of sin is death;" and seeing that children are subject to diseases and death, they must therefore be guilty of sin.

Answer: We confess that death and disease are a consequence of the fall and of Adam's sin; but that this necessarily infers a guilt in all that experience them, we deny. For though the whole outward creation suffered a decay by Adam's fall, according to which it is said in Job that "the heavens are not clean in the sight of God;"[12] yet it does not follow that the herbs, the earth, and the trees are thereby sinners.

---

[12]   Job 15:15

Objection: Lastly, some are so foolish as to object that, if Adam's sin in not imputed to those who actually have not sinned, then it would follow that all infants are saved.

Answer: We are willing that this conclusion be the consequence of our doctrine, rather than accept the unavoidable consequence of theirs, namely, that countless infants eternally perish, not for any sin of their own, but only for Adam's iniquity. Here we are willing to let the controversy stop, commending all to the illuminated understanding of the Christian reader.

CHAPTER II

A Universal Offer of Redemption

Having considered man's fallen, lost, corrupt, and degenerate condition, we must now enquire how, and by what means, he may come to be freed from this miserable and depraved condition.

Absolute Reprobation—A Doctrine of Devils

We must begin by striking at the doctrine of *absolute predestination and reprobation,* whereby many are not afraid to assert that God, by an eternal and immutable decree, has predestinated to eternal damnation the far greater part of mankind, without any regard to their disobedience or sin, but only for the demonstration of the glory of His justice. These miserable souls, they say, are appointed to walk in their own wicked ways, to the end that God's justice may at last lay hold upon them. Not only has He withheld the preaching of the Gospel and the knowledge of Christ from many parts of the world, but even in those places where the gospel is preached, and salvation by Christ is offered, He justly condemns for disobedience great multitudes, from whom He has withheld the grace by which they could have been saved. This, it is said, is because He has, by a secret will unknown to all men, foreordained and decreed (without any respect to disobedience or sin) that many shall not obey, and that the offer of the Gospel shall never prove effectual for their salvation, but only serve to occasion their greater condemnation.

Now, with respect to this horrible and blasphemous doctrine, our view is the same with many others, who have both wisely and learnedly, according to Scripture, reason, and antiquity, refuted it. And seeing that so much has already been written against this doctrine that very little can be added, I shall be brief in this respect. However, because in stands in opposition to my way, I cannot let it altogether pass.

First, we may safely call this doctrine a novelty, seeing that for the first four hundred years after Christ there is no mention made of it. For as it is contrary to the Scripture's testimony, and to the tenor of the Gospel, so all the ancient writers, teachers, and doctors of the church pass it over with profound silence. The first foundations of it were laid in the later writings of Augustine, who, in his warring against Pelagius, let fall some expressions which some have unhappily picked up, to the establishing of this error. Afterwards this doctrine was promoted by Dominicus, a friar, and the monks of his order; and at last unhappily taken up by John Calvin (otherwise a man in some respects to be commended), to the great staining of his reputation, and the defamation of Protestant Christianity. And though it was confirmed by the decrees of the Synod of Dort, it has since lost ground, and is being discredited by most men of learning and piety in all Protestant churches. However, we do not quarrel with it because of the silence of the ancients, the scarcity of its asserters, or the learnedness of its opposers, but because we believe it to have no real foundation in the writings or sayings of Christ and the apostles, and find it highly injurious to God himself, to Jesus Christ our Mediator and Redeemer, and to the power, virtue, nobility, and excellency of His blessed Gospel, and lastly to all mankind.

First, it is highly injurious to God, because it makes Him the author of sin, which of all things is most contrary to His nature. I confess the asserters of this principle deny this consequence; but their denial is pure illusion, seeing that it so naturally follows from their doctrine. For if God has decreed that certain reprobated people shall perish, without any respect to their evil deeds, but only of His own pleasure; and if He has also decreed this long before they had a being, or any capacity to do good or evil, so that they must walk in their wicked ways, by which they are led to condemnation; who then, I ask, is the first author and cause of this but God, who so willed and decreed it? This is the most natural, and indeed the only consequence that can exist. And although many of the preachers of this doctrine have sought out various, strange, strained, and intricate distinctions to defend their opinion, and to avoid this horrid consequence, yet some of the most eminent of them have been so plain in the matter, that they have put it beyond all doubt. I shall instance a few among many of these:

The following are John Calvin's expressions: "By the ordination and will of God, Adam fell. God would have man to fall."[1] "Man is blinded by the will and commandment of God."[2] "We refer the cause of our hardening to God."[3] "The highest or remote cause of hardening is the will of God."[4] "It follows that the hidden counsel of God is the cause of hardening."[5]

Theodor Beza writes: "God has predestined not only unto damnation, but also unto the causes of it, whomsoever He saw fit."[6] "The decree of God cannot be excluded from the causes of corruption."[7]

"It is certain," says Jerome Zanchi, "that God is the first cause of hard-heartedness."[8] "Reprobates are held so fast under God's almighty decree that they cannot help but sin and perish."[9]

"It is the opinion," says David Pareus, "of our doctors, that God did inevitably decree the temptation and fall of man. The creature sins indeed necessarily, by the most just judgment of God. Our men do most rightly affirm that the fall of man was necessary and inevitable, because of God's decree."[10]

---

[1] Calvin in cap. 3. Gen.

[2] Id. 1 Inst. c. 18. s. 1.

[3] Id. lib. de praed.

[4] Idem, lib. de provid.

[5] Id. 3 Inst., cap. 23. s. 1.

[6] Beza, lib. de praed.

[7] Id. de praed. ad art. 1.

[8] Zanchi, de excaecat. q. 5.

[9] Idem, lib. 5 de nat. Dei cap. 2. de praed.

[10] Pareus, lib. 3. de amiss. gratiae. c. 2. ibid., c. 1.

"God," says Ulrich Zwingli, "moves the robber to kill. He kills, God forcing him thereunto. But you will say, he is forced to sin; I confess truly that he is forced."[11]

"Reprobate persons," says Piscator, "are absolutely ordained to this twofold end, to undergo everlasting punishment, and necessarily to sin; and therefore to sin, that they may be justly punished."[12]

Such sayings do plainly and evidently make God the author of sin. Some have sought to evade this necessary consequence with the assertion that men sin *willingly;* but this does not help them at all, since man's willingness and propensity to evil is, according to their own judgment, necessarily imposed upon him by the will and decree of God. This shift is just as if I should take a child who is incapable of resisting me, and throw it down from a great precipice. The weight of the child's body indeed makes it go readily down, and the violence of the fall does immediately kill it. Now then, I ask you, though the child goes down willingly because of the weight of its body, and not by any immediate stroke of my hand (who am perhaps at a great distance away when he is killed)—am I or the child the proper cause of its death? Therefore, let any man of reason judge, if the above citations not only make God the immediate author of sin, but also more unjust than the most unjust of men.

Secondly, this doctrine is injurious to God because it makes Him delight in the death of sinners, yes, and to desire many to die in their sins, contrary to many scriptures, such as: "'As I live,' says the Lord God, 'I have no

---

[11] Zwingli, lib. de prov. c. 5.
[12] Resp. ad Vorst. part 1, p. 120.

pleasure in the death of the wicked, but that the wicked turn from his way and live. Turn, turn from your evil ways! For why should you die, O house of Israel?'"[13] And, "For this is good and acceptable in the sight of God our Savior, who desires all men to be saved and to come to the knowledge of the truth."[14] And, "The Lord is not slack concerning His promise, as some count slackness, but is long-suffering toward us, not willing that any should perish but that all should come to repentance."[15] But if God has created men that He might show forth His justice and power in them, as these men affirm, and for the effecting of this He has not only withheld from them the means of doing good, but also predestined the evil that they might fall into it—certainly He must necessarily delight in their death, and will them to die, seeing He does nothing against His own will.

Thirdly, it is highly injurious to Christ our mediator, and to the efficacy and excellency of His Gospel; for it renders His mediation ineffectual—as if He had not by His sufferings thoroughly broken down the middle wall, nor yet removed the wrath of God, nor purchased the love of God towards all mankind—if it was indeed foreordained that His death would be of no service to the far greater part of mankind.

Fourthly, it makes the preaching of the Gospel a mere mockery and illusion, if indeed many of those to whom it is preached are, by an irrevocable decree, excluded from benefitting by it. It makes the preaching of faith and repentance wholly useless, along with all of the Gospel promises

---

[13]   Ezekiel 33:11

[14]   1 Timothy 2:4

[15]   2 Peter 3:9

and warnings. For, to what purpose are these, if all is dependent upon a former decree by which a chosen man cannot fail to be saved at the appointed time (though it be at the last hour of his life), and a reprobate man cannot fail to be damned, though he seek and wait upon the Lord with diligence?

Fifthly, it is injurious to the coming of Christ and His propitiatory sacrifice, which the Scripture affirms to have been the fruit of God's love to the world, and transacted for the sins and salvation of all men. For, if the coming of Christ was foreordained to save very few, and also served to harden and augment the condemnation of the far greater number of men who do not believe in it (they not being able to believe in it by foreordination), then the cross rather serves as a testimony of God's wrath to the world, and as an act of indignation towards the majority of mankind.

Sixthly, this doctrine is highly injurious to mankind, for it renders them in a far worse condition than the devils in hell. For devils once stood in their proper domain, and had the capacity so to remain; these then suffer for their own rebellion and guilt. But, according to this doctrine, many millions of men are forever tormented for Adam's sin, of which they know nothing, and for which they bear no responsibility. Indeed, this renders them worse than the beasts of the field, of whom their master requires no more than they are able to perform. And when a beast is killed, death to them is the end of their sorrow; but those chosen for damnation are forever tormented for not doing that which they were never able to do. Yes, this puts man into a far worse condition than Pharaoh put the Israelites; for though he withheld straw from them, yet by much labor and pain there was a possibility of obtaining it. But this doctrine makes God withhold all means of salvation, so that man can by no means attain it!

Christ's Death For All Men

Having thus briefly removed this false doctrine which stood in my way, I come to the matter of our proposition, which is, "That God, out of His infinite love, who delights not in the death of a sinner but that all should live and be saved, has sent His only begotten Son into the world, that whosoever believes in Him might be saved." The truth of this statement, being almost entirely in the express words of Scripture, will not require much proving. And because our assertion here is in common with many others who have both earnestly and soundly, according to the Scripture, pleaded for God's offer of universal redemption,[16] I shall be brief until I come to those assertions which are more singularly and peculiarly ours.

---

[16] Editor's Note: There have been many misunderstandings and false conclusions derived from the Quakers use of the term "universal" in reference to redemption. This word was used by Friends to establish an intentional contrast with the prevalent idea that God offers the saving knowledge of Christ to only a small, predestined few. The Quakers rejected the idea of individual predestination and a "limited atonement," insisting that Christ died for all men, and that an offer of redemption extends towards all the sons of Adam. It is this gracious, inward invitation that is universal. When received, followed, and obeyed, the light of Christ becomes the life and salvation of the soul. When rejected, the same light becomes man's eternal condemnation. See John 3:19-21. Early Quakers were not at all proponents of universalism, or universal reconciliation.

This truth of Christ's dying for all men is of itself so evident from the Scripture testimony that there is scarce found any other article of the Christian faith so frequently, so plainly, and so positively asserted. It is that which makes the preaching of Christ to be truly termed the Gospel, or an announcement of glad tidings to all. Thus the angel declared the birth and coming of Christ to the shepherds, saying, "Behold, I bring you good tidings of great joy, which shall be *to all people;*"[17] notice he says not to a few people. Now if this coming of Christ had not brought a possibility of salvation to all, this announcement should rather have been accounted bad tidings of great sorrow to most people; nor would the angel have had reason to sing, "Peace on earth and good will towards men"[18] if the greatest part of mankind had been necessarily shut out from receiving any benefit by it. And why would Christ have sent out His disciples to "preach the Gospel to every creature?"[19] Indeed, He commanded them to preach repentance, remission of sin, and salvation to every son and daughter of mankind, warning every man and exhorting every man, as Paul did in Col. 1:28.

Now, how could these ministers of Christ have preached the Gospel to every man, "in much assurance,"[20] if salvation by that Gospel was not possible to all? What if some had asked them, "Has Christ died for me?" To this, those who deny the universal death of Christ can answer nothing, and only run in a circle. But "the feet of those that

---

[17]   Luke 2:10

[18]   Luke 2:14

[19]   Mark 16:15

[20]   1 Thessalonians 1:5

bring the glad tidings of the Gospel of peace" are said to be "beautiful,"[21] for they preach a common salvation, repentance unto all, the offering of a door of mercy and hope to all through Jesus Christ "who gave himself a ransom for all."[22] Yes, the Gospel invites all; and certainly Christ did not intend to deceive and delude the greater part of mankind when He invited and cried out, saying, "Come unto Me all you that labor and are heavy laden and I will give you rest."[23] If all then ought to seek after Him, and to look for salvation by Him, He must necessarily have made salvation possible to all. Certainly it would be mere mockery to bid men seek what is impossible to obtain. And those who deny that by the death of Christ salvation is made possible to all men, do most blasphemously make God mock the world; for they admit that God has given His servants a commission to preach the Gospel of salvation unto all, and yet they maintain He has previously decreed it impossible for most to receive it.

But seeing that Christ, after He arose and perfected the work of our redemption, gave a commission to preach repentance, remission of sins, and salvation to all, it is manifest that He indeed died for all. For He that has commissioned His servants thus to preach is a God of Truth, and not a mocker of poor mankind, nor does He require of any man that which is simply impossible for him to do.

Moreover, if we regard the testimony of the Scripture in this matter, there is not one scripture that I know of that plainly affirms Christ did not die for all, though there are

---

21 Isaiah 52:7, Romans 10:15

22 1 Timothy 2:6

23 Matthew 11:28

many that positively and expressly assert He did, such as: "Therefore I exhort first of all that supplications, prayers, intercessions, and giving of thanks be made for all men... For this is good and acceptable in the sight of God our Savior, who desires all men to be saved and to come to the knowledge of the truth... who gave Himself a ransom for all, to be testified in due time."[24] Nothing could more plainly confirm what we have asserted; for first the apostle here recommends them to "pray for all men," and then, as though seeking to prevent any objections as to the will of God in this regard, tells them that "it is good and acceptable in the sight of God, who desires all men to be saved." He then manifests the reason for His willingness that all men should be saved, in these words: "Who gave himself a ransom for all." It is as if he said, 'Since Christ died for all, and since He gave himself a ransom for all, He therefore desires all men to be saved.' And Christ Himself shows God's love to the world in these words, "God so loved the world that He gave His only begotten Son, that whosoever believes in Him should not perish but have everlasting life."[25] This word "whosoever" is an indefinite term, from which no man is excluded.

The same is very positively affirmed in these words, "But we see Jesus, who was made a little lower than the angels, for the suffering of death crowned with glory and honor that He, by the grace of God, should taste death for every man."[26] Clearly, if He "tasted death for every man" then there is no man for whom He did not taste death, nor

---

[24] 1 Timothy 2:1, 3-4, 6

[25] John 3:16

[26] Hebrews 2:9

is there any who may not become a sharer in the benefit of it; for He came not "to condemn the world but that the world might be saved through Him."[27] "He came not to judge the world but to save the world."[28] But according to the doctrine of our adversaries, He came not with the intention to save, but rather to judge and condemn the greater part of the world, contrary to His own express testimony.

And as the apostle Paul (in the words above cited) does positively assert that God desires the salvation of all, so the apostle Peter asserts the same thing negatively—that God "is not willing that any should perish." He writes, "The Lord is not slack concerning His promise, as some count slackness, but is long-suffering toward us, not willing that any should perish but that all should come to repentance."[29] This corresponds with the words of Ezekiel: "'As I live,' says the Lord God, 'I have no pleasure in the death of the wicked, but that the wicked turn from his way and live.'"[30] Therefore, if it is safe to place our trust in God, we cannot believe He intends to deceive us by all of these clear expressions from His servants. And if His manifest will for our salvation has not taken effect, the blame must be on our part, as shall afterwards be shown.

Besides these things, how should we understand the multitudes of earnest invitations, serious accusations, and regretful lamentations that fill the pages of holy Scripture?

---

[27] John 3:17

[28] John 12:47

[29] 2 Peter 3:9

[30] Ezekiel 33:11

Such as, "Why should you die, O house of Israel!"[31] "Why will you not come unto Me, that you might have life?"[32] "I have waited to be gracious unto you;"[33] "I have sought to gather you;"[34] "I have knocked at the door of your hearts;"[35] "Is not your destruction of yourselves?"[36] "I have called all the day long."[37] If those who are so invited by the Lord are really under no capacity of being saved, then we must suppose God to be like the author of a romance or comedy, who amuses Himself by raising the affections and passions of men, sometimes leading them into hope and sometimes into despair, while all along having predetermined what the conclusion will be.

Moreover, this doctrine is abundantly confirmed by the words of the apostle John: "And if anyone sins, we have an Advocate with the Father, Jesus Christ the righteous. And He Himself is the propitiation for our sins, and not for ours only but also for the whole world."[38] The way by which our adversaries seek to avoid this plain testimony is most foolish and ridiculous: suggesting that the "world" here refers only to the world *of believers*. To support this, they have nothing but their own assertion; for let them show me, if they can, in all the Scripture where "the whole world" is taken to mean believers only. I can show them

---

[31] Ezekiel 18:31, 33:11

[32] John 5:40

[33] Isaiah 30:18

[34] Matthew 23:37

[35] Revelation 3:20

[36] Jeremiah 2:17, etc.

[37] Isaiah 65:2

[38] 1 John 2:1-2

where it many times means the contrary.[39]

Furthermore, the apostle, in this very place, makes a distinction between the world and the saints, saying "And not for ours only but for the sins of the whole world." What does the apostle mean by "ours" here? Is he not plainly speaking of the sins of believers? And is not "the whole world" necessarily then a reference to those outside of the church, for whom Christ also died, and to whom the gospel invitation is extended? But we need no better interpreter for the apostle than himself, for he uses the very same expression in the fifth chapter of the same epistle, saying, "We know that we are of God, and the whole world lies in wickedness."[40] Seeing then that the apostle John tells us plainly that Christ not only died for the saints and members of the church of God to whom he wrote, but also for the whole world, let us then hold it for a certain and undoubted truth, despite the squabbles of those who oppose.

The same might also be proved from many more Scripture testimonies, if it were needful. And indeed, all the Fathers of the church (so-called), for the first four centuries, preached this doctrine. These boldly held forth the Gospel of Christ and the efficacy of His death, inviting and entreating the heathen to come and be partakers of the benefits of it. They did not tell them that God had predestinated any of them to damnation, or had made salvation

---

39 Barclay's Note: Such as, "The world knows Me not." "The world receives Me not." "I am not of this world." Besides all these scriptures: Ps. 17:14; Isa. 13:11; Matt. 18:7; John 7:7, 8:26, 12:19, 14:17, 15:18-19, 17:14, and 18:20; 1 Cor. 1:21, 2:12, and 6:2; Gal. 6:14; James 1:27; 2 Pet. 2:20; 1 John 2:15, 3:1, and 4:4-5, and many more.

40 1 John 5:19

impossible to them by withholding the power and grace necessary to believe; but rather declared that a door had been opened for all mankind to come and be saved through Jesus Christ.

Seeing then that this doctrine of the universality of Christ's death is so certain and agreeable to the Scripture's testimony and to Christian antiquity, it may be wondered how so many (some of whom have been esteemed not only learned, but also pious) have been capable of falling into so gross and strange an error? There are indeed a few difficult texts which the unrenewed mind may easily twist and mis-construe, but the principle cause arises from a general mis-understanding of the way or method by which the virtue and efficacy of Christ's death is offered to all men. Here men have stumbled, and resorted to various theological inventions. Not understanding this way, some have departed from clear Scripture testimony, and (as we have seen) limited Christ's atonement to a predestined few. Others have erred in the other direction, affirming that those who have never heard the outward proclamation of Christ are not obliged to believe in Him, or that all are saved regardless of faith in, and obedience to the gospel.

The Seed, Light, and Grace of God

Even as the darkness of the great apostasy did not come upon the Christian world all at once, but rather by several degrees, one thing making way for another, until that thick and gross veil came to be overspread (with which the nations were so blindly covered from the seventh and eighth, until the sixteenth century); and even as the darkness of night does not come upon the outward creation all at once, but by degrees, according as the sun declines in the horizon; so neither did the full and clear light and knowledge of the glorious dispensation of the Gospel of Christ reappear in the world all at once. Indeed, the work of the first witnesses in the reformation was more to testify against and uncover the abuses of the apostasy, than to establish the Truth in purity. He that comes to build a new city, must first remove the old rubbish before he can see to lay a new foundation; and he that comes to a house that is greatly polluted and full of dirt, will first sweep away and remove the filth before setting up his own good and new furniture. The light at dawn is sufficient to dispel the darkness, and to make us see the things that are most conspicuous; but a clear discovering and discerning of things, so as to make certain and perfect observations, is reserved for the arising of the sun and its shining in full brightness.

Now, from certain experience we can boldly affirm, that many an unhappy and hurtful mistake among the Protestants has arisen from a failure to wait for the further rising of this sun; and thus they have built with and among much old Catholic rubbish before the foundation was thoroughly purged. But now, in this our age, the Lord God has seen fit to communicate and make known again a more full, evident, and perfect knowledge of His everlasting Truth and evangelical dispensation (notwithstanding various testimonies to it have been borne by noted persons in several ages, as shall hereafter be seen.) And in order to magnify the glory of His grace, and preclude all cause for boasting, He has raised up a few despicable and uneducated men, for the most part tradesmen, to be the messengers of it. By this Gospel, all the above-mentioned scruples, doubts, hesitations, and objections are easily and evidently answered, and the justice as well as mercy of God, according to their divine and heavenly harmony, are exhibited, established, and confirmed. It is according to this certain Light and Gospel, as the knowledge thereof has been manifested to us by the revelation of Jesus Christ in us, fortified by our own sensible experience, and sealed by the testimony of the Spirit in our hearts, that we can confidently affirm, and clearly declare, according to the testimony of the holy Scriptures, the following points:

I. That God, who out of His infinite love sent His Son, the Lord Jesus Christ, into the world to taste death for every man, has given to every man—whether Jew or Gentile, Turk or Scythian, Indian or Barbarian, of whatsoever nation, country, or place—a certain day or time of visitation, during which it is possible for them to be saved, and to partake of the fruit of Christ's death.

II. That for this end God has communicated and given unto every man a measure of the Light of His own Son, a measure of grace, or a measure of the Spirit, which the Scripture expresses by several names: as sometimes "the seed of the kingdom;"[1] the "Light that makes all things manifest;"[2] the "Word of God;"[3] or "manifestation of the Spirit given to profit withal;"[4] "a talent, or mina"[5] "a little leaven;"[6] "the Gospel preached in every creature."[7]

III. That God, in and by this Light and Seed, invites, calls, exhorts, and strives with every man in order to save him. As this is received, and not resisted, it is able to work the salvation of all—even those who are ignorant of the historical death and sufferings of Christ, and of Adam's fall—by bringing them to a sense of their own misery, to be sharers in the sufferings of Christ inwardly, and by making them partakers of His Resurrection, in becoming holy, pure, and righteous, and recovered out of their sins. By this

---

[1] Matthew 13:18-19

[2] Ephesians 5:13

[3] Romans 10:17

[4] 1 Corinthians 12:7

[5] Matthew 25:15, Luke 19:11

[6] Matthew 13:33

[7] Colossians 1:23, Literal Translation "εν παση τη κτισει"

same Light and Seed, salvation is worked in those who do have the outward and historical knowledge of Christ, opening their understanding rightly to use and apply the things described in the Scriptures, and to receive the saving benefit of them. Nevertheless, this gift of grace may be resisted and rejected in both, in which then God is said to be resisted[8] and pressed down,[9] and Christ to be again crucified, and put to open shame in and among men;[10] and to those who thus resist and refuse Him, He becomes their condemnation.[11]

Now then, according to this doctrine: *First:* The mercy of God is excellently exhibited, in that none are necessarily shut out from salvation; and His justice is demonstrated, in that He condemns none but those to whom He truly made an offer of salvation, having affording them the means sufficient for it.

Secondly: This doctrine, if well considered, will be found to be the foundation of true Christianity, salvation, and real assurance.

Thirdly: It agrees and fits with the whole tenor of the Gospel promises and threats, and with the nature of the ministry of Christ, according to which, the Gospel, salvation, repentance are commanded to be preached to every creature, without respect of nations, kindred, families, or tongues.

Fourthly: It magnifies and commends the merits and

---

[8]   See Acts 7:51; Hebrews 2:3; Galatians 2:21, etc.

[9]   See Amos 2:13

[10]   Hebrews 6:6

[11]   John 3:19

death of Christ, in that it not only accounts them sufficient to save all, but declares them to be brought so near to all men as to thereby put them into the real capacity of salvation.

Fifthly: It exalts the grace of God above all, as the source of all that is truly good—from the least and smallest motions of good, to the whole conversion and salvation of the soul.

Sixthly: It contradicts, overturns, and disables, the false doctrine of those who exalt the light of man's nature, and the strength of man's will, in that it wholly excludes the natural man from having any place or portion in his own salvation, by any acting, moving, or working of his own, until he be first quickened, raised up, and moved by God's Spirit.

Seventhly: Even as it makes the whole of man's salvation solely and completely to depend upon God, so it also makes man's condemnation wholly and in every respect to be of himself. For the man who refuses and resists the gift of God that wrestles and strives with his heart, is forced at length to acknowledge the just judgment of God in afterwards rejecting and forsaking him.

Eighthly: It takes away all ground of despair, and gives every man a ground of hope and a certain assurance that they can be saved. However, it feeds nobody in a false security, for none are certain how soon their day may expire. It is therefore a constant incitement and provocation, and a lively encouragement to every man, to forsake evil and turn to that which is good.

Ninthly: It wonderfully commends the Christian religion among unbelievers, manifesting its truth to all, in that this doctrine is confirmed and established by the experience of all men. For there was never yet a man found in any place of the earth, however barbarous and wild, who has not acknowledged that at some time or other, less or more, he has found something in his heart reproving him for some evil things that he has done. This inward witness is the same in all—both threatening a certain horror as man continues in evil, and also promising and communicating a certain peace and sweetness as grace is given way to and not resisted.

Tenthly: It wonderfully shows the excellent wisdom of God, by which He has made the means of salvation so universal and comprehensive. He is therefore not bound to make use of outward miracles, the ministry of angels, or other unusual means, seeing that, according to this most true doctrine, the Gospel reaches all, of whatsoever condition, age, or nation.

Eleventhly: It is really and effectively (though perhaps not in so many words, yet by deeds) established and confirmed by all the preachers and promoters of Christianity in all the world. For although in their judgment they may oppose this doctrine, they nevertheless preach to every individual that they may be saved, entreating and desiring them to believe in Christ, who has died for them, telling them Jesus Christ calls and wills them to believe and be saved, and that if they refuse, they shall therefore be condemned, and that their condemnation is of themselves. Indeed, such is the evidence and virtue of Truth, that it constrains its adversaries, even against their wills, to plead for it.

Further Considerations upon the Above Propositions

I. First, by this day and time of visitation which, we say, God gives unto all, during which they may be saved, we do not mean the whole course of every man's life—though to some it may be extended even to the very hour of death, as we see in the example of the thief converted upon the cross. Rather, we understand this time of visitation as a season of the Spirit's striving with man for the salvation of his soul (to some shorter, and to others longer, according as the Lord in His wisdom sees fit), which more than sufficiently exonerates God of every man's condemnation. Moreover, it is evidently possible for men to outlive this day or time of visitation, after which there is no possibility of salvation to them. These God justly allows to be hardened as the due punishment for their unbelief, and at times even raises them up as instruments of wrath, and makes them a scourge one against another.[12]

This doctrine is clearly expressed by the apostle in Romans 1, from verse 17 to the end, but especially verse 28, "And even as they did not like to retain God in their knowledge, God gave them over to a debased mind, to do those things which are not fitting." And that many may outlive this day of God's gracious visitation unto them, is shown by the example of Esau, who had the birthright once, and certainly could have kept it; but afterwards, when he wanted to inherit the blessing, he was rejected.[13] This appears also by Christ's weeping over Jerusalem, saying, "If you had

---

[12] Barclay's Note: To men in this condition may be fitly applied those Scriptures which are often wrongly used to prove that God incites men necessarily to sin.

[13] Hebrews 12:16-17

known, even you, especially in this your day, the things that make for your peace! But now they are hidden from your eyes."[14] This plainly demonstrates there was a time when they might have known these things, which time now was removed from them, though they were yet alive.

II. Secondly, we say that there is a Seed, or measure of grace, a Word of God, or Light, by which every man is enlightened (having been given a measure of it), which strives with them in order to save them, and which may, by the stubbornness and wickedness of man's will, be quenched, bruised, wounded, pressed down, slain and crucified. Now, we do not understand this to be the proper essence and nature of God, strictly taken, which is not divisible into parts and measures, but is a most pure, simple being, void of all composition or division; and in this sense He cannot be resisted, hurt, wounded, crucified, or slain by all the efforts and strength of men. But we understand this Seed to be a spiritual, heavenly, and invisible emanation in which God (as Father, Son and Spirit) dwells —a measure of whose divine and glorious life is sown in all men, and which, of its own nature, draws, invites, and inclines to God. And this we call the spiritual flesh and blood of Christ, which came down from heaven, upon which all the saints do feed, and are thereby nourished to eternal life. And as every unrighteous thought or action is witnessed against and reproved by this Light and Seed, so, by such wicked actions it is said to be wounded, crucified, or slain, and so draws back or flees from them.

Now, because this Seed is never separated from God,

---

14   Luke 19:42

but wherever it is, God and Christ are as wrapped up therein, in this respect we say that, when the Seed is resisted, then God is resisted; and where it is borne down, God is said to be pressed, as a cart under sheaves,[15] and Christ is said to be slain and crucified in men.[16] And on the contrary, as this Seed is received in the heart, and allowed to bring forth its natural and proper effect, Christ comes to be formed and raised. The Scripture makes frequent mention of this, calling it "the new man,"[17] "Christ formed within,"[18] or "Christ within, the hope of glory."[19] And this is that Christ within of whom we so often speak and declare, preaching Him, and exhorting people to believe in the Light, and obey it, that they may come to know Christ in them to deliver them from all sin.

But by preaching this Light or Seed within, we do not at all intend either to equal ourselves to the Lord Jesus Christ, who was born of the virgin Mary, and in whom all the fullness of the Godhead dwelt bodily, nor to destroy the reality of His present existence. For, though we affirm that Christ dwells in us, His presence in us is in measure, through the mediation of His Seed. But in that holy Man, the Lord Jesus Christ, the eternal Word (which was with God, and was God) dwelt in fullness and without mediation. He then is as the head, and we are as the members; He is the vine, and we are the branches.

---

[15] Amos 2:13
[16] Hebrews 6:6
[17] Ephesians 4:24; Colossians 3:10
[18] Galatians 4:19
[19] Colossians 1:27

III. Thirdly, we understand this Seed, Light, or Grace to be a real spiritual substance, which the soul of man is capable to feel and apprehend, and from which a real, spiritual, inward birth in believers arises, which is called in Scripture the new creature, or the new man in the heart. This seems strange to carnally minded men because they are not acquainted with it, but we know it, and are sensible of it, by true and certain experience. Indeed it is impossible for a man in his natural wisdom to comprehend it until he comes to feel it in himself, and then he finds that holding it as a mere notion does but little avail him. Yet, though men deny it, we are able to make it appear to be true, and to show that our faith concerning it is not without solid ground. For it is in and by this inward and substantial Seed in our hearts, as it comes to receive nourishment, and to have a birth in us, that we come to have those spiritual senses raised by which we are made capable of tasting, smelling, seeing, and handling the things of God. For a man cannot reach unto these things by his natural spirit and senses, as is above declared.

IV. Fourthly, by insisting upon these things, we do not hereby intend, in any way, to lessen or derogate from the atonement and sacrifice of Jesus Christ; but on the contrary, we do magnify and exalt it. For as we believe all things which are recorded in the holy Scriptures concerning the birth, life, miracles, sufferings, resurrection and ascension of Christ, so we also do believe that it is the duty of everyone to whom these truths have been declared to believe the same. Indeed, we look upon it as damnable unbelief *not* to believe whenever these things have been rightly presented. For the holy Seed that is sown in man, when minded, does lead and incline every heart to believe the truths of Scripture as they are made known. For though it does not reveal in every heart the outward and historical knowledge of Christ, yet it always assents to it whenever it is declared.

And as we firmly believe it was necessary that Christ should come, so that by His death and sufferings He might offer up Himself a sacrifice to God for our sins, who Himself "bore our sins in His own body on the tree;"[20] so we believe that the remission of sins, which any partake of, is only in, and by virtue of, that most satisfactory sacrifice, and not by any other way; for it is "through one Man's righteous act that the free gift has come upon all to justification."[21]

We moreover affirm, that even as all men partake of the fruit of Adam's fall by reason of that evil seed which through him is communicated unto them, making them prone and inclined unto evil, even though millions are ignorant of Adam's fall, never having heard of his eating the forbidden fruit—so also, many may come to feel the influence of this holy and divine Seed and Light, and be turned from evil to good by it, though they know nothing of Christ's coming in the flesh, through whose obedience and sufferings this gift is purchased for them. And, as we affirm it to be absolutely needful that those do believe the history of Christ's outward appearance, to whom it pleased God to bring the knowledge of it; so we do freely confess, that even the outward knowledge is very comforting to such as are

---

[20]   1 Peter 2:24
[21]   Romans 5:18

subject to, and led by the inward Seed and Light. For, not only does hearing of Christ's love and sufferings tend to humble them, but they are thereby also strengthened in their faith, and encouraged to follow that excellent pattern which He has left us, "who suffered for us," as says the apostle Peter, "leaving us an example that we should follow his steps."[22] Indeed, many times we are greatly edified and refreshed with the gracious sayings which have proceeded from His mouth. The history then is truly profitable and comforting when known together with the mystery, and never without it. But the mystery may be profitable without the explicit and outward knowledge of the history.

V. But fifthly, this brings us to another question, namely—whether Christ is therefore in all men? We have said before that a divine, spiritual, and supernatural Light has been given to all men; that God and Christ dwell in it and are never separated from it; and also that, as this is received and yielded to in the heart, Christ comes to be formed and brought forth. But we are far from ever having said that Christ is received by all men, and much less formed in all men; for that is a great attainment, for which the apostle travailed that it might be brought forth in the Galatians. Neither is Christ in all men by way of union, or indeed, to speak strictly, by way of dwelling or inhabiting; because this inhabiting implies a union, or the manner in which Christ resides in the saints. As it is written "I will *dwell* in them, and *walk* in them."[23]

However, in a more general sense, seeing that Christ

---

[22]   1 Peter 2:21

[23]   2 Corinthians 6:16

never is, nor can be, separate from that holy pure Seed and Light which testifies in all men, it may thus be said that He is in all. As observed previously, it is in this sense the Scripture says God is pressed down as a cart under sheaves (Amos 2:13), and that Christ is crucified in the ungodly (Hebrews 6:6)—though to speak properly and strictly, neither can God be pressed down, nor Christ, as God, be crucified. But in this respect, we can direct all men to seek Christ within, who lies crucified in them by their sins and iniquities, that they may "look upon Him whom they have pierced,"[24] and repent. Then, He who now lies slain and buried in them (so to speak), may come to be raised, and have dominion in their hearts over all. In this way also the apostle Paul preached to the Corinthians and Galatians concerning "Christ crucified in them," (*en humin* as the Greek has it.)[25] This Jesus Christ was that which the apostle desired to know in them, and make known unto them, that they might come to be sensible how they had been resisting and crucifying Christ, and that so they might repent and be saved. And because Christ is called "the true Light, that enlightens every man,"[26] "the Light of the world,"[27] this Light is therefore taken to be Christ, who truly is the fountain of all light, and has His dwelling in it forever. Thus the Light of Christ is sometimes called

---

[24] Zechariah 12:10

[25] "For I determined not to know anything in you except Jesus Christ and Him crucified." 1 Corinthians 2:2; "O foolish Galatians! Who has bewitched you that you should not obey the truth, before whose eyes Jesus Christ was clearly portrayed in you as crucified." Galatians 3:1

[26] John 1:9

[27] John 8:12

Christ, i.e., that in which Christ is, and from which He is never separated.

VI. Sixthly, it will clearly appear by what is above said, that we do not understand this divine Seed or Light to be any part of man's nature, nor to be any relic of any good which Adam lost by his fall; for we know it to be a distinct and separate thing from a man's soul and all the faculties of it. Yet such is the malice of our adversaries, that they do not cease to reproach us, as if we preached up a natural light, or the light of man's natural conscience. But we certainly know that the Light of which we speak is not only distinct, but of a different nature from the soul of man, and all of its operations and capacities.

We do not deny that man, as he is a rational creature, has reason as a natural faculty of his soul, by which he can discern things that are rational. Indeed, this is a property natural and essential to him, by which he can know and learn many arts and sciences, beyond what any other animal can do by mere animal faculties. Nor do we deny that man, by this rational principle, may apprehend in his brain and his notions, a knowledge of God and spiritual things; yet this not being the right organ for true spiritual knowledge, it cannot profit him towards salvation, but often rather hinders him. And truly, the great cause of the apostasy has been that man has sought to comprehend the things of God in and by this natural and rational principle, and to build up a religion in it, neglecting and overlooking the Light and Seed of God in the heart. Thus has Antichrist, "exalted himself" in every man, "taking his seat in the temple of God, displaying himself as being God."[28] For men being "the temple of the Holy Spirit,"[29] as the apostle says, whenever the natural reason sets itself up there, above the Seed and Light of God, to reign and rule as a prince in spiritual things (while the holy Seed is wounded and bruised), there is Antichrist in every man, or something exalted above and against Christ.

Nevertheless, we do not hereby suggest that man has received his reason to no purpose, or that it is of no service to him: not at all. For we look upon reason as fit to order and rule man in natural things. And even as God gave two great lights to rule the outward world, the sun and moon, the greater light to rule the day, and the lesser light to rule the night; so He has given man the Light of His Son, a spiritual divine Light, to rule him in things spiritual, and the lesser light of reason, to rule him in things natural. And even as the moon borrows her light from the sun, so ought men, if they would be rightly and comfortably ordered in natural things, to have their reason enlightened by this divine and pure Light. For we confess that, in those that obey and follow this true Light, their enlightened reason may be useful to man even in spiritual things, so long as it is still subservient and subject to the other; even as the biological life in man, when regulated and ordered by his reason, helps him in going about things that are rational.

We do further rightly distinguish the Light of Christ from man's natural conscience; for conscience, being that in man which arises from the natural faculties of man's soul, may be defiled and corrupted. The apostle Paul,

---

[28] 2 Thessalonians 2:4

[29] 1 Corinthians 3:16

speaking of the impure, expressly says, "Even their mind and conscience is defiled."[30] However, this Light can never be corrupted or defiled, nor did it ever consent to evil or wickedness in any; for it is expressly said that it "makes all things manifest that are reprovable,"[31] and so is a faithful witness for God against every unrighteousness in man.

Now conscience, to define it truly, comes from the Latin *conscire*, and is that knowledge which arises in man's heart from what agrees with, or is contrary to, anything believed by him, whereby he becomes conscious to himself that he transgresses by doing something he is persuaded he ought not to do. So then, when the mind has been blinded or defiled with a wrong belief, there arises a conscience from that belief, which troubles him when he goes against it. For example, when a Muslim, who has possessed himself with a false belief that it is unlawful for him to taste wine, acts against his belief and drinks, his conscience smites him for it; but if he keeps many concubines, his conscience does not trouble him, because his judgment is already defiled with a false opinion that it is lawful for him to do the one, and unlawful to do the other. However, if the Light of Jesus Christ in him were minded, it would reprove him, not only for committing fornication, but would also inform him (as he became further obedient to it) that Muhammad is an impostor, just as Socrates, in his day, was informed by it of the falsity of the heathens' gods.

Likewise, if a Roman Catholic were to eat meat during Lent, or not be sufficiently diligent in the adoration of saints and images, his conscience would smite him for it,

---

[30]   Titus 1:15
[31]   Ephesians 5:13

because his judgment is already blinded with a false belief concerning these things. However, the Light of Christ never consented to any of those abominations. So then, man's natural conscience is sufficiently distinguished from it; for conscience follows the judgment; it does not inform it. But this Light, as it is received and obeyed, removes the blindness of false judgment, opens the understanding, and rectifies both the judgment and conscience. Thus we confess that conscience is an excellent thing, wherever it is rightly informed and enlightened from above. Indeed, some of us have fitly compared it to a lantern, and the Light of Christ to the candle within. A lantern is useful when a candle burns and shines brightly within it, but otherwise it is of no use. It is therefore to the Light of Christ *in the conscience*, and not to man's natural conscience, that we continually commend men. This is their certain guide unto life eternal.

Lastly, this Light, Seed, etc., is seen to be no power or natural faculty of man's mind, because a healthy man can, when he pleases, stir up, move, and exercise the faculties of his soul; indeed, he is master of them, and except there be some natural cause or impediment in the way, he can use them at his pleasure. But this Light and Seed of God in man cannot be moved and stirred up when man pleases; rather it moves, blows, and strives with man as the Lord sees fit. For though there be a possibility of salvation extended to every man during the day of his visitation, yet man cannot, at any time when he pleases, or whenever he has a sense of his misery, stir up that Light and Grace so as to procure for himself real tenderness of heart. Instead, he must wait for it, as it comes upon all at certain times and seasons, working powerfully upon the soul, mightily tendering and breaking it. At such a time, if a man does not resist it, but receives and follows it, he comes to know salvation by it. Even as the pool of Bethesda did not cure all, but only those who waited for the stirring of the waters, so God, at certain times, moves in love to mankind by His Seed in their heart, setting their sins in order before them, seriously inviting them to repentance, and offering them remission of sins and salvation; which, if a man accepts, he may be saved.

Now, there is no man alive, and I am confident there never shall be, who, if they will deal faithfully and honestly with their own hearts, will not be forced to acknowledge that they have been sensible of this in some measure, less or more; which is a thing that man cannot bring upon himself with all his pains and industry. This then, O man and woman, is the day of God's gracious visitation to your soul, and you shall be happy forever if you resist it not. This is the day of the Lord, which, as Christ says, is like the lightning, which shines from the east unto the west, and like the wind or spirit, which blows upon the heart, and no man knows where it comes from, or where it goes.

The Seed's Operation in the Heart

VII. Seventhly, this leads me to speak concerning the manner of this Seed or Light's operation in the hearts of all men, which will show even more clearly how we vastly differ from all those who exalt a natural power or light in man, and how our principle leads, above all others, to attribute our whole salvation to the mere power, Spirit, and grace of God.

Some have presented us with the following question: If two men have equal and sufficient Light and Grace, and the one is saved by it, and the other not, is not then the will of man the true cause of the one's salvation, beyond the other? To this question we answer: that as the Grace and Light in all is sufficient to save all, and of its own nature would save all, so it strives and wrestles with all to save them. He that resists its striving is the cause of his own condemnation; he that does not resist, finds it to become his salvation. So then, in the one that is saved, the working is of the grace, and not of the man, and this is in his yielding and passiveness, rather than his acting. However, afterwards, as a man is wrought upon by the grace, there is a will raised in him by which he comes to be a coworker with the grace; for as Augustine has said, "He that made us without us, will not save us without us."

Thus, the first step is not by man's working, but by his *not* working contrary to the Light and Grace of God. And during these seasons of every man's visitation, though man is wholly unable, of himself, to work with the grace, nor to move one step out of his natural condition until grace lays hold upon him, yet it is possible for him to be passive and not resist it, or to be stubborn and resist it. So we say, the grace of God works in and upon man's nature, which, though of itself wholly corrupt and defiled, and prone to evil, yet, is capable to be wrought upon by the grace of God —even as iron, though a hard and cold metal of itself, may be warmed and softened by the heat of the fire, and wax melted by the sun. And, as iron or wax, when removed from the fire or sun returns to its former condition of coldness and hardness, so man's heart, as it resists or retreats from the grace of God, returns to its former condition again. I have often had the manner of God's working towards the salvation of all men illustrated to my mind by one or two clear analogies, which I shall here add, for the information of others.

The first is of a man greatly diseased, to whom I compare man in his fallen and natural condition. Now, some suppose that God, the great physician, offers medicine to this poor man only after he has done all in his power, by any skill or knowledge of his own, to secure his own health. These are those that say, if a man improve his reason or natural faculties, then God will see fit to supply grace. Others say that God comes and makes on offer of a remedy to the sick man, but leaves it to the liberty of the man's will either to receive it or reject it. But we say, that He, even the Lord, this great physician, comes and pours the remedy into the sick man's mouth and lays him in his bed, so that, if the sick man be but passive, it will necessarily work the cure. But if he is stubborn and troublesome, and insists upon rising up and going forth into the cold, and eating such foods as are hurtful to him while the medicine should operate; then, though of its nature the medicine tends to cure him, yet it will prove destructive to him in the end. So then, in this example, the man who perishes would certainly be the cause of his own death; and the man who is cured would owe his health wholly to the physician, and not to any deed of his own.

The second example is of several men lying in a dark pit together, where all their senses are so stupefied that they are scarcely sensible of their own misery. To this I compare man in his natural, corrupt, and fallen condition.

Again, we do not understand that God looks down and, upon seeing one doing all in his power to deliver himself, decides that such a one deserves to be assisted. Nor do we suppose that a deliverer comes to the top of the pit, puts down a ladder, and expects them to ascend in their own strength, understanding, and will. Instead, we believe that the deliverer comes at certain times, and fully discovers and informs the men of the great misery and hazard they are in if they continue in that horrid and unhealthy place. Indeed, this deliver forces them to a certain sense of their misery, (for even the wickedest of men are at times are made sensible of their misery by God's visitation), and not only so, but at times lays hold upon them, and gives them a pull, in order to lift them out of their misery—which if they do not resist, will save them; only they may resist it.

These two examples, in some measure, do illustrate the matter, showing that the grace of God reaches all, though its effect differs according to the object it meets with. For this grace is a ministration of mercy and love in all those that do not reject it, but receive it (John 1:12); but the same is a ministration of wrath and condemnation, in those that do reject it (John 3:19); even as the sun, by one act or operation, melts and softens wax, but dries and hardens clay. The nature of the sun is to cherish the creation, and therefore the living are refreshed by it, and the flowers send forth a good savor as it shines upon them, and the fruits of the trees are ripened. However, with a dead carcass, a thing without life, the same rays of the sun will cause it to stink, and putrefy it. So then, every man, during the day of his visitation, is shined upon by the sun of right-eousness, and capable of being influenced by it, so as to send forth good fruit, and a good savor, and to be melted by it. But when a man has rejected the light, and has sinned out his day, then the same sun hardens him, as it does the clay, and makes his wickedness more to appear and putrefy, and send forth an evil savor.

CHAPTER IV

THE PROOF OF OUR POSITION

Having then clearly and evidently stated the issues and given our mind and judgment in these matters, so it will it make our proof both the easier and the shorter.

A Day or Time of Visitation

The first thing to be proved is that God has given to every man a day or time of visitation, wherein it is possible for him to be saved. If we can prove that there is a day and time given in which some might have been saved, who actually perished, the matter is done. But this clearly appears by the many regrets and complaints expressed by the Spirit of God throughout all the Scriptures, even to those that did perish; blaming them for having not accepted or received God's visitation and offer of mercy to them.

In this way the Lord did express Himself in the beginning to Cain, saying "Why are you angry? And why has your countenance fallen? If you do well, will you not be accepted? And if you do not do well, sin lies at the door."[1] This was said to Cain before he slew his brother Abel, when

---

[1]   Genesis 4:6-7

the evil seed had begun to tempt him and work in his heart. Here we see how God gave a warning to Cain in season, in the day of His visitation towards him, offering him acceptance and remission if he did well; for this question "Will you not be accepted?" implies the affirmative, "You will be accepted, if you do well." So then, if we can trust God Almighty, the fountain of all Truth and equity, then it was possible for a time even for Cain to be accepted. For surely God would not have proposed the doing of good as a condition, if He had not also given to Cain sufficient power whereby he was enabled to do it.

This the Lord also shows in giving a day of visitation to the old world: "And the Lord said, 'My Spirit shall not always strive in man;'" (for so it ought to be translated).[2] This manifestly implies that His Spirit *did* strive with man, and *does* strive with him for a season, which season expires when God ceases to strive with them in order to save them. And it is during this day of visitation given to all men that God is said to "wait to be gracious,"[3] and to be "long-suffering"[4] towards His creation. The apostle Peter says expressly that the "long-suffering of God waited in the days of Noah for those of the old world,"[5] which being compared with Gen. 6:3, before mentioned, does sufficiently support our proposition. And that none may object that this long-suffering or striving of the Lord was not in order to save them, the same apostle expressly says that "the long-suf-

---

[2]   בָּ אָ דָ ם —i.e. "in man"

[3]   Isaiah 30:18

[4]   Exodus 34:6; Numbers 14:18; Psalms 86:15; Jeremiah 15:15, etc.

[5]   1 Peter 3:20

fering of God is to be accounted salvation;"[6] for, as he affirms a little before (vs. 9), "God is not willing that any should perish."

In the following verse, Peter further refers to the writings of Paul, showing this to have been the universal doctrine of the church. And it is observable what he adds upon this occasion, how there are some things in Paul's epistles which are hard to understand, which the unstable and unlearned twist to their own destruction, most likely insinuating Paul's expressions from Romans 9. Many indeed, who are unlearned in spiritual things, have made Paul's words contradict the truth of God's long-suffering towards all and His will that not any should perish, but all be saved. If only these had give more heed to Peter's warning!

But the place in Paul's writings which Peter seems here most particularly to hint at, does much contribute also to clear up the matter. For Paul writes: "Or do you despise the riches of His goodness, forbearance, and long-suffering, not knowing that the goodness of God leads you to repentance?"[7] Here he speaks to the unregenerate and to the wicked, who in the following verse he says "are treasuring up wrath unto the day of wrath." But to such as these he commends the riches of the forbearance and long-suffering of God, showing that the tendency of God's goodness leads men to repentance. How could it necessarily tend to lead them to repentance, and how could it be called riches or goodness to them, if there were not a time wherein they might repent and come to be sharers of the riches offered by it?

---

[6]   2 Peter 3:15
[7]   Romans 2:4

From all which I thus argue: If God pleads with the wicked from the possibility of their being accepted; if God's Spirit strives in them for a season in order to save them, though they afterwards perish; if He waits to be gracious to them; if He is long-suffering towards them, and this long-suffering (while it endures) is unto salvation, during which time God does not will them to perish, but exhibits to them the riches of His goodness and forbearance in order to lead them to repentance—then I conclude, there is a day of visitation given to men wherein they may be saved, if they repent.

Moreover, the same appears from the prophet Isaiah, where it is said: "What more could have been done to My vineyard that I have not done?" For in the second verse he says: "He dug it up and cleared out its stones, and planted it with the choicest vine. He built a tower in its midst, etc." And yet, when "He expected it to bring forth good grapes, it brought forth wild grapes."[8] Therefore he calls the inhabitants of Jerusalem and the men of Judah to judge between Him and His vineyard, saying; "What more could have been done to My vineyard that I have not done in it?" This parable was applied to many in Israel who refused God's mercy in the days of the kings, and the same example was used by Christ (Matt. 21:33; Mark 12:1; Luke 20:9). Here Jesus shows that a vineyard was planted, and that all things necessary were given to the workers in order to gather fruit to repay their master. The master many times waited to be merciful to them, sending servants after servants, and passing by their many offenses, before determining at last to destroy and cast them out. Now then, this

---

[8]   Isaiah 5:2

parable could not have been spoken with reference to the saints, or to those who repent and are saved; for it says expressly, "He will destroy them." Nor is it reasonable to suggest that these men were not in a capacity to have done good, for the Lord's expectation was plain, and indeed He says through the prophet "What more could I have done?" So then, it is more than manifest by this parable (repeated in three gospels) that Christ holds forth His long-suffering towards men, even in their wickedness, for a time, affording them a true means of salvation; and that those who nevertheless resist, do so to their own condemnation. See also the following parallel scriptures: Prov. 1:24-26; Jer. 18:9-10; Matt. 18:32-34; Acts 13:46.

Lastly, that there is a day of visitation given to the wicked wherein they might have been saved, and which, having expired, they are shut out from salvation, appears evidently by Christ's lamentation over Jerusalem, expressed in three separate places (Matt. 23:37; Luke 13:34; and 19:41-42): "Now as He drew near, He saw the city and wept over it, saying, 'If you had known, even you, especially in this your day, the things that make for your peace! But now they are hidden from your eyes.'" And "O Jerusalem, Jerusalem, the one who kills the prophets and stones those who are sent to her! How often I wanted to gather your children together, as a hen gathers her brood under her wings, but you were not willing!" What could more evidently prove our doctrine? For first, He insinuates that there *was* a day wherein the inhabitants of Jerusalem might have known those things that belonged to their peace. And secondly, He manifests that during that day He was willing to have gathered them, even as a hen gathers her chicks. This illustration shows plainly that the offer of salvation made to them was not in vain on His part, but was as real, and with as great cheerfulness and willingness as a hen gathers her chicks. Indeed, even as a hen shows love and care towards her brood, such is the care of Christ to gather lost men and women, to redeem them out of their corrupt and degenerate state. Then thirdly, it is seen how, because they refused, the things belonging to their peace were hidden from their eyes. And why were they hidden? Because they would not allow Him to gather them; they would not see those things that were good for them in the season of God's love towards them. And therefore, that day having expired, they could not see them; and so God permitted them to be hardened in unbelief.

So it is *after* real offers of mercy and salvation are rejected, that men's hearts are hardened, and not before. Thus that saying is verified, "Whoever has, to him more will be given; but whoever does not have, even what he has will be taken away from him."[9] This may seem a riddle, yet it is easily solved according to this doctrine. He has not, because he has lost the season of using what he had, and so to him it is now to him as nothing. For Christ uses this expression (Matt. 25:26) upon the occasion of taking the one talent from the slothful servant, and giving it to him that was diligent—which talent was in no way insufficient of itself, but was of the same nature with those given to the others. Therefore the Lord had reason to expect the profit of it proportionably, as well as from the rest.

So I say, it is after the rejecting of this day of visitation, that the judgment of hardness is inflicted upon men

---

9   Mark 4:25

and women, even as Christ pronounced it upon the Jews (quoting from Isaiah 6:9, of which all four evangelists make mention: Matt. 13:14; Mark 4:12; Luke 8:10; John 12:40). And the apostle Paul, after he had offered the Gospel of salvation to the Jews at Rome, makes mention of the same, saying, "The Holy Spirit spoke rightly through Isaiah the prophet to our fathers, 'Go to this people and say: "Hearing you will hear, and shall not understand; and seeing you will see, and not perceive; for the hearts of this people have grown dull. Their ears are hard of hearing, and their eyes they have closed, lest they should see with their eyes and hear with their ears, lest they should understand with their hearts and turn, so that I should heal them.'"[10] So it again appears that God desired them to see, but having closed their eyes, they are therefore justly hardened.

Of this matter Cyril of Alexandria speaks well, in answering the following objection: "But some may say, if Christ has come into the world that those who see may be blinded, then their blindness is not to be imputed unto them; but rather to Christ, who is the cause of their blindness. But such as these speak irrationally, who are not afraid to call God the author of evil. For as the natural sun is carried upon our horizon that it may communicate the gift of its clearness unto all, and make its light shine upon all, yet if anyone close his eyelids, or willingly turn himself from the sun, refusing the benefit of its light, he lacks its illumination, and remains in darkness. This, no doubt, is through no the defect of the sun, but through his own fault.

In the same way, Christ, the true Sun, came to enlighten those that sat in darkness, and in the region of

---

[10]   Acts 28:24-27

the shadow of death, that He might communicate unto all the gift of knowledge and grace, and illuminate the inward eyes of all by His own spiritual splendor. But many reject the gift of this heavenly Light freely given to them, having closed the eyes of their minds, lest so excellent an illumination of the eternal Light should shine unto them. It is not then through defect of the true Sun that they are blinded, but only through their own iniquity and hardness; for, as the wise man has said, 'their wickedness has blinded them.'"[11]

From all which I argue: If there was a day wherein the obstinate Jews might have known the things that belonged to their peace, which, because they rejected them, were hid from their eyes; and if there was a time wherein Christ would have gathered some who, because they refused, could not be gathered; then those who might have been saved, do actually perish, because they have slighted the day of God's visitation towards them.

A Measure of Saving Light and Grace Given to Man

That which must next be proved is the way by which God seeks to work salvation in man during the day of his visitation, which is through a measure of saving, sufficient, and supernatural Light and Grace given to every man. This I shall prove, by God's assistance, with several plain and clear testimonies of the Scripture.

First, from John 1:9: "That was the true Light which gives light to every man coming into the world." This scripture does so clearly favor us, that it is called by some "the

---

[11]   John, lib. 6, cap. 21.

Quakers' text"—for it so plainly demonstrates our position that there is scarcely need for either interpretation or deduction. Indeed, this verse is itself something of a conclusion which follows two previous assertions, namely, that "In Him was life, and the life was the light of men," and "The Light shines in the darkness, and the darkness did not comprehend it."

Let us first observe that this apostle calls Christ the "Light of men," and gives this to us as one of His chief properties. And the same apostle says elsewhere that it is as we walk with Him in that Light (which He communicates to us), that we come to have fellowship and communion with Him.[12] Secondly, we are told that "this Light shines in darkness, though the darkness did not comprehend it." And thirdly, that this is the "true Light which gives light to every man coming into the world." Here the apostle, being directed by God's Spirit, has carefully avoided that notion of our adversaries, who would restrict this Light to a certain number of individuals. For, where it says "every man," there is clearly no man excluded. And should they be so obstinate (as sometimes they are) as to say that this "every man" is only every one of the elect, then the following words, "every man coming into the world," does invalidate their objection. Therefore, it is here plainly asserted that no man comes into the world whom Christ has not enlightened in some measure, and in whose dark heart this Light does not shine. Though the darkness does not comprehend it, still it shines there, and its nature is such as would dispel the darkness, whenever men do not shut their eyes upon it. Indeed, the purpose for which this

---

[12] 1 John 1:7

Light is given is expressed in verse 7—"that all men, through it [that is, through the Light], might believe."[13]

Seeing then that this Light is the Light of Jesus Christ, and is said to be the Light through which men come to believe, I think it need not be doubted that it is a supernatural, saving, and sufficient[14] Light. If it were not supernatural, it could not properly be called the Light of Jesus. And surely the Light which enlightens man cannot be any of the natural gifts or faculties of his soul, because it is said to "shine in the darkness,"[15] and cannot be comprehended by it. Now this "darkness" is no other than man's natural condition and state, in which natural state he can easily comprehend, and does comprehend, those things which are

---

[13] Barclay's Note: *di' autou* (through it) does very well agree with *photos* (the Light), as being the nearest antecedent; though many translators have made it relate to John (to make it suit with their own doctrine), as if all men in the world were to believe through John. But all could not believe through John, because all men could not know of John's testimony; whereas every man being enlightened by this Light may through it come to believe. John shined not in the darkness; but this Light shines in the darkness, so that, having dispelled the darkness, it may produce and beget faith. And it is by walking in this Light that we have this communion and fellowship, not by walking in John, which is nonsense. So that this relative *di' autou* must necessarily refer to the Light *(photos),* of which John bears witness, so that through that Light, with which Christ has enlightened every man, all men might come to believe.

[14] Editor's Note: i.e. sufficient for the salvation of the soul. Some adversaries of early Friends, while admitting that the Light of Christ is given in measure to every man, insisted that this is a measure or endowment *insufficient* to save the soul. These argued that there is a *common grace* (or illumination) by which all men possess moral discernment between good and evil, and then a separate and *saving grace,* which is bestowed upon Christians only.

[15] 2 Corinthians 4:6

common to him as man. But that man in his natural condition is called darkness, see Ephesians 5:8: "For you were once darkness, but now you are light in the Lord." and several other places, such as Acts 26:18, Colossians 1:13, and 1 Thessalonians 5:5, where the condition of man in his natural state is termed "darkness." Therefore, I say, this Light that shines in darkness cannot be any natural property or faculty of man's soul, but must be the supernatural gift and grace of Jesus Christ.

And that this Light is sufficient and saving is apparent in that it was given "that all men through it may believe." Moreover, we are told that, by walking in it, we enjoy fellowship with the saints, and "the blood of Jesus Christ cleanses us from all sins."[16] And that which we are commanded to believe in, in order "to become the children of Light," must certainly be a supernatural, sufficient, and saving principle; for Christ has said, "While you have the Light, believe in the Light, that you may become the children of the Light."[17]

Some object that by "Light" here, the disciples were meant to understand Christ's *outward* person, in which He desired them to believe. Now, we do not deny that they ought to have believed in Christ's outward appearance, acknowledging Him to be the Messiah who was to come. But how this could be the intent of Christ's words in this place I do not see. For the words "while you have the Light," and those of the previous verse, "Walk while you have the Light lest darkness come upon you," clearly imply that, when that Light in which they were to believe was

---

[16]   1 John 1:7
[17]   John 12:36

removed, then they should lose the capacity or season of believing. This could not be understood of Christ's outward appearance, since many did savingly believe in Him (as do all Christians at this day) when His bodily presence or outward man was far removed from them. So that this Light in which they were commanded to believe must be that inward, spiritual Light, that shines in their hearts for a season, even during the day of man's visitation. While this Light continues to call, invite and exhort, men are said to have it and may believe in it; but when men refuse to believe in it, and reject it, then it ceases to be a Light to show them the way, and leaves the sense of their unfaithfulness as a sting in their conscience, which is a terror and darkness unto them and in which they cannot know where to go. Therefore, to such rebellious ones as these, the "day of the Lord" is said to be "darkness and not light."[18]

So then, it appears that, though many do not receive the Light (as the darkness does not comprehend it), nevertheless this saving Light shines in all that it might save them. Concerning this, Cyril of Alexandria has spoken well:

"With great diligence and watchfulness," he says "does the apostle John endeavor to anticipate and prevent the vain thoughts of men. He had just now called the Son the true Light, by whom he affirmed that every man coming into the world was enlightened; yes, and that He was in the world and the world was made by Him. One might then object, 'If the Word of God is the Light, and if this Light enlightens the hearts of men and suggests unto them piety and a

---

[18] Amos 5:18

true understanding of things, and if He was always in the world and was the creator or builder of the world, then why was He so long unknown unto the world?' It might seem to follow that, because He was unknown to the world, the world was therefore not enlightened by Him, nor was He totally Light. But let not man accuse the Word of God and His eternal Light, but rather his own weakness: for the Son enlightens, but the creature rejects the grace that is given to it and abuses the clearness of understanding granted it by which it might have known God. Like the prodigal, man has turned his sight to the creation, neglecting to go forward, and through laziness and negligence has buried God's illumination and despised His grace. And it was in order to avoid this very thing that the Thessalonians were commanded by Paul to watch and be sober.

Therefore, the fault must be imputed to the wickedness of those who are illuminated, and not to the Light; for though the sun rises upon all, yet he that is blind receives no benefit by it. None can accuse the brightness of the sun, but will ascribe the cause of not seeing to the blindness; and such is the case with the only begotten Son of God, for He is the true Light and sends forth His brightness upon all. But the god of this world, as Paul says, has blinded the minds of those that do not believe (2 Cor. 4:4), lest the Light of the Gospel shine unto them.

We say then, that darkness is come upon men, not because they are altogether deprived of Light, but because man is dulled by an evil habit and become worse, and has made the measure of grace in some respect to languish. By these words, then, the world is accused as ungrateful and insensible, not knowing its Author, nor bringing forth the good fruit of their illumination. So it seems it may now be truly said of all, what was of old said by the prophet of the Jews "I expected it to have brought forth good grapes, but it brought forth wild grapes."

From this it appears Cyril believed that a saving illumination is given unto all, and that it is of the same kind with that grace of which Paul makes mention to Timothy, saying, "Neglect not the grace that is in you."

Now, that this saving Light and Seed, or a measure of it, is given to all, Christ tells us expressly in the parable of the sower (Matt. 13:18; Mark 4, and Luke 8:11). He says that the "seed" which is sown in those several sorts of grounds is the "Word of the Kingdom," which the apostle calls the "Word of faith,"[19] or the "implanted Word which is able to save the soul;"[20]—which words imply that it is of a saving nature, and that in good soil it bears fruit abundantly.

Let us then observe that this Seed of the Kingdom—this saving, supernatural, and sufficient Word—was really sown in the stony ground, the thorny ground, and by the wayside, where it did not profit but became useless as to these grounds. This was, I say, the very same Seed that was sown in the good ground. It is then (according as Christ Himself interprets the parable) the fear of persecution, the deceitfulness of riches, the cares of the world, and desires

---

[19]   Romans 10:8

[20]   James 1:21 — "*ho logos emphutos*"

for other things, which hinder this Seed from growing in the hearts of many. It is not a lack of sufficiency in its own nature, for it is the same that grows up and prospers in the hearts of those who receive it. So then, it is manifest that though all are not saved by it, yet there is a seed of salvation planted and sown in the hearts of all by God, which seed would grow up and redeem the soul if it were not choked and hindered.

Concerning this parable, Victor of Antioch (on the fourth chapter of Mark) says, "Our Lord Christ has liberally sown the divine Seed of the Word and offered it to all without respect of persons. As he that sows distinguishes not between ground and ground, but simply casts the seed without distinction, so our Savior has offered the food of the divine Word to all, although He was not ignorant what would become of many. Indeed, He behaved Himself in such a way as He might justly say, 'What should I have done that I have not done?'"

To this corresponds the parable of the talents (Matthew 25), where he that had two talents was accepted as well as he that had five, because the talents were used to the master's profit. And he that had one talent might have done the same, for his talent was of the same nature with the rest, and was equally capable of bringing forth a proportionable increase. So then, though there is not an equal proportion of grace given to all—to some five talents, to some two talents, and to some but one—yet there is given to all that which is sufficient, and no more is required than according to that which is given: "For unto whomsoever much is given, from him shall much be required."[21] He that

---

[21]   Luke 12:48

had the two talents and returned four was equally acceptable to the master as he who had five talents and returned ten. So the man who received one talent would likewise have been accepted in returning two; for no doubt one was capable of producing two, even as the two produced four, and the five produced ten.

Furthermore, this saving, spiritual Light *is* the Gospel, which the apostle expressly says is preached "in every creature under heaven;" even that very "Gospel whereof Paul was made a minister."[22] For the Gospel is not a mere declaration of good things, but rather "the power of God unto salvation, to all those that believe."[23] Though the outward declaration of the Gospel be taken sometimes for the Gospel, yet this is but figuratively and by a metonymy. For to speak properly, the Gospel is the inward power and life which preaches glad tidings in the hearts of all men, offering salvation unto them, and seeking to redeem them from their iniquities. It is therefore said to be preached "in every creature under heaven," though there are many thousands of men and women to whom the outward gospel was never preached.

Therefore the apostle Paul (in Romans 1), where he says "the Gospel is the power of God unto salvation," adds that "therein is revealed the righteousness of God from faith to faith;" and also the "wrath of God against such as suppress the Truth of God in unrighteousness."[24] And it is for this reason that Paul, in the following verse, says "because that which may be known of God is manifest in

---

[22] Colossians 1:23, Literal Translation "εν παση τη κτισει" i.e. "in every creature"

[23] Romans 1:16

[24] Romans 1:17-18

them; for God has shown it to them."[25] So then, that which may be known of God is made known by the Gospel, which was manifest in them. For those of whom the apostle here speaks had no outward gospel preached to them, so that it was by the inward manifestation of the knowledge of God in them (which is indeed the Gospel preached in man) that "the righteousness of God is revealed from faith to faith"— that is, it reveals to the soul that which is just, good, and righteous, and as the soul receives it and believes, righteousness comes more and more to be revealed from one degree of faith to another. For though, as the following verse says, the outward creation declares the power of God, yet that which may be known of Him is manifest within, by which inward manifestation we are made capable to see and discern the Eternal Power and Godhead in the outward creation. So, were it not for this inward Light and Grace, we could no more understand the invisible things of God by the outward visible creation, than a blind man can see and discern the variety of shapes and colors, or judge the beauty of the outward creation. Therefore Paul first says, "That which may be known of God is manifest in them," and in and by *that* they may read and understand the power and Godhead in those things that are outward and visible. Though some might insist that the outward creation does, of itself, without any supernatural or saving Light in the heart, declare to the natural man that there is a God; yet, I say, what would such a knowledge avail if it did not also communicate to me the will and nature of God, and how I might do what is acceptable to Him? For the outward creation, though it may beget a persuasion that

---

25   Romans 1:19

there is some eternal power or virtue by which the world has had its beginning; yet it does not inform me what is just, holy, and righteous, or how I shall be delivered from my temptations and evil affections and come unto right-eousness. Indeed, this must be from some inward manifes-tation in my heart. But these Gentiles, of whom the apostle here speaks, knew to distinguish between good and evil by that inward law and manifestation of the knowledge of God in them, as is demonstrated in the following chapter of Romans.

The prophet Micah, speaking of man in general, declares this: "He has shown you, O man, what is good. And what does the Lord require of you, but to do justly, to love mercy, and to walk humbly with your God?"[26] Notice, he does not speak of God's requirement till he has first assured them that God has shown unto them what is good. Now, it is because this is shown unto all men and is mani-fest in them, that the apostle can say "the wrath of God is revealed against them in that they suppress the Truth in unrighteousness;" that is, they suppress the measure of Truth, the Light, the Seed, the Grace in them, for they "hide their talent in the earth," or in the earthly and unrighteous part in their hearts, and do not allow it to bring forth fruit. Instead, their measure or Seed is choked with the sensual cares of this life, the fears of reproach, and the deceitfulness of riches, as is manifest by the above-mentioned parables.

But the apostle Paul opens and illustrates this matter yet more in Romans 10, where he declares that the Word which he preached "is not far off, but near in the heart and

---

[26] Amos 6:8

in the mouth;" (now the Word which he preached and the Gospel which he preached, and of which he was a minster, is one and the same). He then sets up the common objection of our adversaries in the 14th and 15th verses: "How shall they believe in Him of whom they have not heard? And how shall they hear without a preacher?" And this he answers in the 18th verse, saying, "But, I say, have they not heard? Yes indeed, 'Their sound has gone out to all the earth, and their words to the ends of the world;'"[27] insinuating that this divine Preacher has sounded in the ears and hearts of all men. For, with regard to the outward apostles this saying was not true, neither then, nor for many hundred years after. Indeed, for all we know there may still be nations and kingdoms who have never heard of Christ or his apostles outwardly.

This inward and powerful Word of God is yet more fully described in the epistle to the Hebrews: "For the Word of God is living and powerful, and sharper than any two-edged sword, piercing even to the division of soul and spirit, and of joints and marrow, and is a discerner of the thoughts and intents of the heart."[28] The virtues of this spiritual Word are here enumerated—it is living and powerful, and is a searcher and trier of the hearts of all. No man's heart is exempt from it, for the apostle says, "There is no creature hidden from His sight, but all things are naked and open to the eyes of Him to whom we must give account." Though this ultimately and mediately refers to God, yet it nearly and immediately relates to His Word or Light, which, seeing all, is plainly in the hearts of all.

---

[27]   Romans 10:18, quoting from Psalms 19:4

[28]   Hebrews 4:12

This Word then is that faithful witness and messenger of God that bears witness for God, and for His righteousness in the hearts of all men. For the Lord "has not left man without a witness,"[29] and He is said to be "given for a witness to the people."[30] And as this Word bears witness for God, so it is not placed in men only to condemn them; for He who is given for a witness, says the prophet, is also "given for a leader and commander."[31] The Light is given that all through it may believe,[32] "for faith comes by hearing, and hearing by the Word of God," which is placed in man's heart, both to be a witness for God, and to be a means to bring man to God, through faith and repentance. So this Word is said to be powerful, able to divide between the soul and the spirit. It is like a two-edged sword, that it may cut off iniquity and separate between the precious and the vile. And because man's heart is naturally cold and hard, like iron, therefore God has placed this Word in him, which is said to be "like a fire, and like a hammer."[33] And even as by the heat of the fire, the iron (being naturally cold) is warmed, and by the strength of the hammer it is softened and framed according to the mind of the worker; so the cold and hard heart of man is, by the virtue and power of this Word of God near and in the heart, warmed and softened (when not resisted) in order to receive a heavenly impression and image.

The greater part of the church fathers have spoken at

---

[29] Acts 14:17

[30] Isaiah 55:4

[31] Isaiah 55:4

[32] John 1:7

[33] Jeremiah 23:29

length concerning this Word, Seed, Light, and saving Voice, which calls unto salvation, and is able to save.

Clement of Alexandria says, "The divine Word has cried, calling all, knowing well those that will not obey. And yet, because it is in our power either to obey or not to obey, that none may claim the pretext of ignorance, it has made a righteous call and requires only that which is according to the ability and strength of everyone."[34] The same author, in his Warning to the Gentiles, says "That heavenly ambassador of the Lord—the grace of God that brings salvation—has appeared unto all. This is the new song, coming, and manifestation of the Word which now shows itself in us, which was in the beginning and was first of all." And again, "Hear, therefore, you that are afar off; hear, you who are near; the Word is hid from none, the Light is common to all and shines to all. There is no darkness in the Word, so let us hasten to salvation, to the new birth, that we, being many, may be gathered unto the one true love."

Justin Martyr, in his first apology, says, "that the Word which was and is, is in all; even that very same Word which, through the prophets, foretold things to come."

Salvation by the Inward Working of Grace and Light in the Heart

The third proposition which needs to be proved has two parts: *First,* that it is only by this Light, Seed, or Grace that God works the salvation of men, causing them to partake of the benefit of Christ's death, and the salvation pur-

---

[34] lib. 2, Stromat.

chased by Him; and *second,* that by the working and operation of this same Grace and Light, many have been, and
some may be saved, to whom the Gospel has never been
outwardly preached, and who (because of inescapable cir-
cumstances) are utterly ignorant of the outward history of
Christ.

Having already proved that Christ has died for all, that
there is a day of visitation given to all men during which
salvation is possible unto them, and that God has actually
given a measure of saving Grace and Light unto all,
preached the Gospel to and in them, and placed the Word
of faith in their hearts, the matter of this proposition may
seem already to be proved. Yet, for the further satisfaction
of all who desire to know the Truth and hold it as it is in
Jesus, I shall attempt to prove this from two or three clear
Scripture testimonies, and to remove the most common
objections usually brought against it.

I. As to the first, because it is already granted by most, I
shall try to prove it in just a few words. First from the
words of Christ to Nicodemus, "Most assuredly, I say to
you, unless one is born again, he cannot see the kingdom of
God."[35] Now this birth does not come by the outward
preaching of the Gospel, or by a historical faith in Christ;
for many have this, and firmly believe it, and yet are not
one bit renewed. Indeed, the apostle Paul, in his commen-
dation of the necessity and excellence of this "new creation," goes so far as to lay aside, in a certain respect, the
outward knowledge of Christ, or the knowledge of Him
after the flesh. He says, "Therefore, from now on, we

---

[35]   John 3:3

regard no one according to the flesh. Even though we have known Christ according to the flesh, yet now we know Him thus no longer. Therefore, if anyone is in Christ, he is a new creation; old things have passed away; behold, all things have become new."[36] Here it clearly appears that Paul makes the knowledge of Christ after the flesh to be the mere rudiments, so to speak, which spiritual children learn, and which afterwards, when they have further progressed, are of less use to them, having come to possess the very substance to which the first precepts pointed. Now as all comparisons have their limitations, I shall not affirm this one to hold in every respect; but I believe it will hold in this: that even as those who go no further than the rudiments are never to be accounted learned, so too those who go no further than the outward knowledge of Christ are not to inherit the kingdom of heaven. Yet those who come to know this birth to be Christ indeed, and by it have been made a new creature, having "old things pass away and all things become new," these may safely say with the apostle, "Though we have known Christ according to the flesh, yet now we know Him thus no longer."

Now this new creature proceeds from the work of Christ's Light and Grace in the heart. It is begotten by that Word that is sharp and piercing (of which we have spoken), the implanted Word that is able to save the soul. Christ has purchased for us this holy Seed, that by it a birth might be brought forth; and this the apostle Paul calls "the manifestation of the Spirit given to every one to profit withal."[37]

---

[36]   2 Corinthians 5:16-17

[37]   1 Corinthians 12:7

The apostle Peter also ascribes this birth to the same Seed and Word of God, saying, "Having been born again, not of corruptible seed but incorruptible, through the Word of God which lives and abides forever."[38] Though this Seed be small in its appearance, so that Christ compares it to a "grain of mustard seed, which is the least of all seeds,"[39] and though it be hid in the earthly part of man's heart, yet therein is life and salvation towards the sons of men wrapped up, which comes to be revealed as they give way to it. And in this Seed in the hearts of all men is the Kingdom of God, as in a capacity to be known and exhibited according as it receives depth, and is nourished, and not choked. So it is that Christ said the Kingdom of God was in the very Pharisees[40] who did oppose and resist Him, and were justly accounted as serpents and a generation of vipers. Now the Kingdom of God could be in these men in no other way but as in a Seed, even as the thirty-fold and hundred-fold increase was wrapped up in the small seed that lay on the path, and did not spring forth for lack of nourishment. And just as the whole body of a great tree is wrapped up potentially in the seed of the tree, and so is brought forth in due season; and as the capacity of a man or a woman is not only in a child but even in the very embryo, even so, the Kingdom of Jesus Christ, yes Jesus Christ himself—"Christ within, who is the hope of glory," who becomes wisdom, righteousness, sanctification and redemption—is sown into every man's heart, in that little incorruptible Seed, ready to be brought forth as it is cher-

---

[38]   1 Peter 1:23

[39]   Matthew 13:31-32

[40]   Luke 17:20-21

ished and "received in the love of it."[41] For no men can be said to be worse than those rebellious and unbelieving Pharisees; and yet this Kingdom was as a seed within them, and they were directed to look for it there. So, it is neither "lo here" nor "lo there," in this or the other observation, that the kingdom is known, but only as this Seed of God in the heart is minded and cherished. And certainly, it is because this Light, Seed, and Grace that appears in the heart of man is so little regarded and so much overlooked, that so few know Christ brought forth and formed in them.

The Calvinists look upon grace as an irresistible power and therefore neglect and despise this eternal Seed of the Kingdom in their hearts, deeming it a low, insufficient, and useless thing as to their salvation. On the other hand, the Catholics, Arminians, and Socinians seek to set up their natural power and will, and with one consent deny that this little Seed, this small appearance of the Light, could be that supernatural and saving grace of God given to every man to save him. Consequently, upon them is verified that saying of the Lord Jesus Christ, "This is the condemnation of the world, that Light is come into the world, but men love darkness rather than Light;" and the reason is added, "because their deeds are evil." All confess they feel this condemnation for evil, but they will not allow it to be of the virtue of grace. Some call it reason; others a natural conscience; still others call it a relic of God's image that remained in Adam. Thus Christ, even as He met with opposition from all kinds of professors in His outward appearance, does now meet with the same in His inward appearance. It was the lowness of His outward man that

---

[41]   2 Thessalonians 2:10

made many despise Him, saying, "Is not this the son of the carpenter? Are not His brethren and sisters among us? Is this not a Galilean? And did ever a prophet come out of Galilee?" And other similar reasonings. For they expected an outward deliverer who, as a prince, should deliver them with great ease from their outward enemies, and not such a Messiah as should be crucified shamefully and, as it were, lead them into many sorrows, troubles, and afflictions.

Even so now, the lowness of Christ's inward appearance makes the crafty Jesuits, the rational Socinians, and the learned Arminians overlook Him, desiring instead something upon which they can exercise their subtlety, reason, and learning, and also use the liberty of their own wills. And the secure Calvinists, they would have a Christ to save them without any trouble, to destroy all their outward enemies for them and do nothing or little within, while they meanwhile live securely and at ease in their sins. But when all of this is well examined the cause is plain: it is "because their deeds are evil" that with one consent they reject this Light—for it checks and reproves even the wisest and most learned of them in secret. Indeed, all of their logic cannot silence it, nor can the most secure among them stop its voice from crying and reproving them within for all their confidence in the outward knowledge of Christ. For as we have demonstrated, in a day or time it strives and wrestles with all; and it is the unmortified nature, the first nature, the old Adam, yet alive in the wisest and most learned, in the most zealous for the outward knowledge of Christ, that denies this, despises it, and shuts it out to their own condemnation. These then fall under the description: "For everyone practicing evil hates the light and does not come to the light, lest his deeds should be exposed."[42] Therefore, it can now be said from true and certain experience, even as it was said of old, "The stone which the builders rejected, has become the chief cornerstone."[43]

Glory to God forever, who has arisen again to plead with the nations, and therefore has sent us forth to preach this everlasting Gospel unto all—Christ near to all, the Light in all, the Seed sown in the hearts of all, that men may come and apply themselves to it. And we rejoice that we have been made to lay down our wisdom and learning (such of us as have had some of it) and our carnal reasoning, to learn of Jesus and sit down at His feet in our hearts and hear Him, who there makes all things manifest and reproves all things by His Light.[44] For many are wise and learned in notions, in the letter of the Scripture, as the Pharisees were, and can speak much of Christ and plead strongly against infidels, Turks, and Jews, and perhaps against some heresies, who in the meantime are crucifying Christ in the small appearance of His Seed in their hearts. Oh it would be far better to be stripped and naked of all, and account it all as dross and dung, and become a fool for Christ's sake! Then they would know Him to teach them in their hearts; they would witness Him raised there, feel the virtue of His cross there, and say with the apostle, "God forbid that I should boast except in the cross of our Lord Jesus Christ, by whom the world has been crucified to me,

---

[42] John 3:20

[43] Psalms 118:22; Matthew 21:42; Mark 12:10; Luke 20:17; Acts 4:11

[44] Ephesians 5:13

and I to the world."[45] This is better than to write thousands of commentaries and to preach a multitude of sermons.

And truly, it is because of the operation of this cross in our hearts that we have denied our own wisdom and wills in many things, and have forsaken the vain worships, fashions, and customs of this world. For these several centuries the world has been full of a dry, fruitless, and barren knowledge of Christ, feeding upon the husk and neglecting the kernel, following after the shadow but strangers to the substance. The devil cares not how much of this lifeless knowledge abounds, provided he can still possess the heart and rule in the will, crucifying the appearance of Christ there, and so keep the Seed of the Kingdom from taking root. Indeed, he has led them abroad, saying, "lo here" and "lo there," and has made them wrestle in a false zeal, so often one against another, contending for this or that outward observation, seeking Christ in this and the other external thing, such as bread and wine. Some say it is this way; some say it is another; some say He is in Scriptures and books, some in societies and pilgrimages and merits. And still some, confiding in an external and barren faith, think all is well if they do but firmly believe that He died for their sins—past, present, and to come—while in the meantime Christ lies crucified and slain within them, and is daily resisted and opposed in His appearance in their hearts.

It is from a sense of this blindness and ignorance that is come over Christendom, that we are led and moved of the Lord so constantly and frequently to call all, invite all, request all to turn to the Light in them, to believe in and

---

[45] Galatians 6:14

mind the Light of Christ in them. And in the name, power, and authority of the Lord—not in school arguments and lofty distinctions—we do charge and direct them to lay aside their wisdom, to come down out of that proud, airy, brain-knowledge, to stop their mouth (however eloquent it may appear to the worldly ear), to be silent and sit down as in the dust, and to mind the Light of Christ in their own consciences. If He were thus minded, they would find Him to be a sharp, two-edged sword in their hearts, and as a fire and a hammer that would knock against and burn up all that carnal, gathered, natural stuff, and make even the stoutest of them tremble and become "Quakers" indeed. Alas, those who will not come to feel this now, and to kiss the Son while their day lasts, but instead harden their hearts, will certainly be made to feel the Truth when it is too late. Therefore, as the apostle says, "Examine yourselves as to whether you are in the faith. Test yourselves. Do you not know yourselves, that Jesus Christ is in you?— unless indeed you are disqualified."[46]

The Work of Grace in Those Who Have Not Heard

II. Secondly, that which remains now to be proved is, that by the operation of this Light and Seed, some have been (and may yet be) saved, to whom the Gospel is not outwardly preached, nor the history of Christ outwardly known. To make this easier, we have already shown how Christ has died for all men, and given unto all a measure of saving Light and Grace, so that the Gospel is preached to them, and in them (though not necessarily in any outward

---

[46] 2 Corinthians 3:5

way), leaving all men in a possibility of salvation.

In addition to those arguments which have already been used to prove that all men have a measure of saving grace, I shall now add another: namely, that excellent saying of the apostle Paul to Titus, "For the grace of God that brings salvation has appeared to all men, teaching us that, denying ungodliness and worldly lusts, we should live soberly, righteously, and godly in the present age."[47] Nothing could be more clear than this statement, for it comprehends both parts of the controversy. First, it plainly asserts this to be no natural principle or light, but rather, "the grace of God that brings salvation." Secondly, it says that this has appeared not to a few, but rather to all men. Moreover, the fruit of this grace declares just how powerful it is, seeing that it comprehends the whole duty of man. It teaches us first to forsake evil, to deny ungodliness and worldly lusts; and then it teaches our duty in all things: First, to live soberly, which comprehends temperance, chastity, meekness, and the things that relate to one's self. Secondly, to live righteously, which comprehends equity, justice, and honesty, and those things which relate to our neighbors. And lastly, to live godly, which comprehends piety, faithfulness, and devotion, which are the duties relating to God. So then there is nothing required of man, or needful to man, which this grace does not teach.

Though this might suffice, yet to put it further beyond all question, I shall instance another saying of the same apostle: "Therefore, as through one man's offense judgment came to all men, resulting in condemnation, even so through one Man's righteous act the free gift came to all

---

[47] Titus 2:11

men, resulting in justification of life."[48] From this it can be plainly seen that, even as all men have received a loss from Adam which leads to condemnation, so too all men have received a gift from Christ, which leads to justification. And if this gift of Christ be received and obeyed, then all men, even those who lack the outward knowledge of Christ, may be saved;[49] for Christ was given as a "Light to enlighten the Gentiles, that You should be My salvation to the ends of the earth."[50]

Objection: The most common objection to this doctrine is taken from the words of Peter, "There is no other name under heaven given among men by which we must be saved." Thus the heathen, not knowing this name, cannot be saved.

Answer: Though they do not know His name outwardly, yet they may know the name Jesus (which signifies Savior) inwardly, by feeling the virtue and power of it to free them from sin and iniquity in their hearts. I confess there is no other name by which any can be saved; but salvation lies not in a literal and outward knowledge, but in an experiential knowledge. Those that have the literal knowledge are not saved by it without a real, experiential knowing of

---

[48]   Romans 5:18

[49]   Editor's Note: To this, the following Scripture might be added as further proof: "Judas (not Iscariot) said to Him, 'Lord, how is it that You will manifest Yourself to us, and not to the world?' Jesus answered and said to him, 'If anyone loves Me, he will keep My word [i.e. the implanted Word, Grace, Light]; and My Father will love him, and We will come to him and make Our home with him.'" (John 14:22-23)

[50]   Isaiah 49:6, See also Isaiah 42:6, 60:3; Luke 2:32; Acts 13:47

Jesus. Yet those that have the real, inward knowledge may be saved without the external name, as the arguments hereafter will more fully show. For if the outward knowledge of Christ were necessary before men could receive any benefit from Him, then (by the rule of contraries) it would follow that men could receive no hurt except by the outward knowledge of Adam's fall. But experience proves otherwise; for how many millions have been injured by Adam's fall that know nothing of there ever being such a man in the world, or of his eating the forbidden fruit? Why then may not some be saved by the gift and grace of Christ in them, making them righteous and holy, though they know not distinctly how that gift was purchased for them by the death and sufferings of Jesus who was crucified at Jerusalem—especially in cases where God Himself has made the outward knowledge impossible to them? Many are killed by poison infused into their food, though they know neither what the poison was, nor who infused it. Likewise, many are cured of their diseases by good remedies, though they know not how the medicine is prepared, what the ingredients are, nor oftentimes who made it. The like may also hold in spiritual things, as we shall hereafter show.

Now, even our adversaries readily confess that many infants and mentally disabled persons are saved without the outward knowledge of Christ. Here they break their general rule, and cannot allege that it is because such are free from sin, seeing they also affirm that all infants, because of Adam's sin, deserve eternal condemnation, as being really guilty in the sight of God. And with mentally disabled people, experience shows us that they are subject to many common iniquities as well as other men.

Objection: If it be said, that these children are the children of believing parents:

Answer: What then? None of them dare say that parents transmit grace to their children. And do they not all affirm that the children of believing parents are guilty of original sin, and deserve death as well as others?

Objection: And if they should further allege that these children are within the bosom of the visible church, and are partakers of the sacraments:

Answer: All of this gives no certainty of salvation; for (as all Protestants confess) these sacraments do not confer grace independently of the faith of the recipient. And will they not also acknowledge that there are many others in the bosom of the visible church, who are clearly no members of it?

But if our opposers are willing to extend this charity towards infants and mentally disabled persons, so that these are judged capable of salvation because they are under a simple impossibility of knowing the means of salvation, what reason can be alleged why the like charity should not be extended to such as *are* capable of knowing, yet have never heard the outward and historical gospel? Is not a man in China, or in India, as much to be excused for not knowing a thing which he never heard of, as the disabled person who cannot hear, or the infant who cannot understand?

But the truth of our doctrine manifestly appears by that saying of Peter in Acts, "Of a truth I perceive that God is no respecter of persons. But in every nation, he that fears Him and works righteousness, is accepted of Him."[51] Peter was before liable to that mistake which the rest of the Jews were in—judging that all were unclean except themselves, and that no man could be saved, except as they were converted to their religion and circumcised. But God showed Peter otherwise in a vision, teaching him to call nothing common or unclean which God had cleansed. And therefore, seeing that God had regarded the prayers of Cornelius, who was a stranger to the outward law, and to Jesus Christ, Peter found that God had accepted him. And as Cornelius is said to have feared God before he had this outward knowledge, therefore Peter concludes that everyone, in every nation, without respect of persons, who fears God and by Him works righteousness, is accepted of Him. Now we have already proved that to every man a measure of grace is given whereby he may live godly and righteously. Thus we see that by this grace Cornelius did so, and was accepted, and that his prayers came up for a memorial before God, even before he had this outward knowledge.

Also, was not Job "a perfect and upright man, that feared God, and shunned evil?"[52] Who taught Job these things? How did he know of Adam's fall?[53] And from what Scripture did he gain that excellent knowledge and faith by which he knew that his Redeemer lived? Most believe him to have lived before Moses, so must it not have been an

---

[51] Acts 10:34-35

[52] Job 1:1

[53] Job 31:33

inward grace in the heart that taught Job to shun evil and fear God? Notice how he reproved the wickedness of men (chapter 24). And after he recounted their wickedness, does he not condemn them for "rebelling against the Light," and for "not knowing its way, or abiding in the paths?"[54] It appears then that Job believed men had a Light, and that because they rebelled against it, they therefore knew not its ways, nor abode in its paths. And also Job's friends, though in some things they erred, yet who taught them all the excellent sayings and knowledge which they had? Did not God give it to them in order to save them? Who taught Elihu that "There is a spirit in man, and the breath of the Almighty gives him understanding."[55] Or that, "The Spirit of God has made me, and the breath of the Almighty gives me life?"[56] And did not the Lord at last accept a sacrifice for them?[57] Who dares then say that they are damned?

But the apostle puts this controversy out of doubt, for, if we may believe his plain assertion, he tells us that some Gentiles indeed "did the things contained in the law."[58] From all of which I argue as follows:

- *In every nation, he that fears God and works righteousness is accepted.*

- *But some of the heathen did fear God, and wrought righteousness by Him.*

---

54 Job 24:13

55 Job 32:8

56 Job 33:4

57 Job 42:8

58 Romans 2:14

- *Therefore they were accepted.*

Can there be anything more clear? And this appears even more plain by another verse, taken out of the same chapter (v. 13). The words are, "The doers of the Law shall be justified." From which I thus argue, from plain Scripture:

- *The doers of the Law shall be justified*

- *But some of the Gentiles did the things contained in the Law, showing that the work of the Law was written in their hearts.*[59]

- *Therefore these were justified.*

Paul, through that whole chapter, labors as if he were contending now with our adversaries, in order to confirm this doctrine. He says, "Tribulation and anguish on every soul of man who does evil, of the Jew first and also of the Gentile; but glory, honor, and peace to everyone who works what is good, to the Jew first and also to the Greek. For there is no partiality with God."[60] Here the apostle clearly approves Peter's words to Cornelius (before mentioned), showing that both they that have an outward law and they that have none, when they do good[61] shall be justified. So then, unless we think Paul did not mean what he clearly spoke, we may safely conclude that such Gentiles as

---

[59] Romans 2:15

[60] Romans 2:9-11

[61] Editor's Note: By "doing good" Barclay does not refer to the so-called good works of fallen man, but to the good which results from receiving and yielding to the inward manifestations of the Grace, Light, or Seed of God (as previously explained) by which the soul is brought out of sin and corruption and made a new creation.

these were justified, and did partake of that "honor, glory, and peace, which comes upon every one that does good."[62] And so we see that, even as the presence of the outward knowledge of Christ cannot save without the inward, neither can the lack of outward knowledge condemn those who have the inward. And in these scriptures it appears that many who have lacked the outward, have indeed come to a knowledge of the gospel inwardly, by virtue of the work of that Grace and Light given to every man. By the operation of this grace, received and heeded, these Gentiles forsook iniquity and grew in true righteousness and holiness (as was proved above). Though they knew not the history of Adam's fall, yet they were sensible in themselves of the loss that came by it, feeling their inclination to sin, and the power of the "body of sin"[63] working in them. And likewise, though they knew not the outward coming of Christ, yet they were sensible of that inward power and salvation which came by Him, both before and since His appearance in the flesh.

Lastly, I question whether those who insist upon the outward knowledge of Christ for salvation can prove that all the patriarchs and fathers before Moses had any distinct knowledge either of Adam or Christ. For seeing how Moses most certainly wrote of Adam by revelation, it is doubtful whether the patriarchs before him knew anything of the history of the tree of the knowledge of good and evil, or of Adam's eating the forbidden fruit; and far less of the Christ, that He should be born of a virgin, crucified, raised, etc.

---

[62]   Romans 2:10

[63]   Romans 6:6

A Few Examples Among Ancient Writers

Thus we see that it is the inward work, and not the outward history and Scripture, that gives true knowledge, and by this inward Light many of the Gentile philosophers were sensible of the loss received by Adam, though they did not know the outward history. Hence Plato asserted that, "Man's soul was fallen into a dark cave, where it only conversed with shadows." Pythagoras says, "Man wanders in this world as a stranger, banished from the presence of God." And Plotinus compares "man's soul, fallen from God, to a cinder, or dead coal, from which the fire is extinguished." Some of them said that "the wings of the soul were clipped or fallen off, so that they could not flee unto God." These, and many more expressions might be gathered out of their writings to show that they were not without a sense of their loss, and the great fall of man from presence of God.

These also had a knowledge and discovery of Jesus Christ inwardly, as a remedy in them, to deliver them from that evil seed, and the evil inclinations of their own hearts, though not using these specific names. Some called Him a Holy Spirit, as Seneca, who said, "There is a Holy Spirit in us that treats us as we treat Him."[64] Cicero calls it an "innate light, constant and eternal, calling unto duty by commanding, and deterring from deceit by forbidding."[65] He further adds that this light "cannot be abrogated, nor can any be freed from it, neither by senate nor people; for it is one, eternal, and the same always to all nations, so that

---

[64] Epist. 41
[65] De Republica, cited by Lactantius (6 Instit.)

there is not one at Rome and another at Athens. Whosoever does not obey it must seek to flee from himself, and in this he is greatly tormented, though he should escape all other punishment." Plotinus also calls Him Light, saying that "as the sun cannot be known but by its own light, so God cannot be known but by His own Light. And as the eye cannot see the sun but by receiving its image, neither can man know God but by receiving His image. Thus it behooves man to come to purity of heart before he can know God." He elsewhere calls Him "Wisdom," a name frequently given Him in Scripture—see Prov. 1:20 to the end; and Prov. 8:9-34, where Wisdom is said to cry, entreat, and invite all to come unto her and learn of her. And what is this Wisdom but Christ? Accordingly, those among the heathen who came to forsake evil and cleave to righteousness, were called "philosophers," that is, lovers of wisdom. They knew this wisdom was near to them, and that "the best knowledge of God and divine mysteries was by the inspiration of the wisdom of God."

Much more of this kind might be instanced, by which it appears that some of these men knew Christ, and by His working in them were brought from unrighteousness to righteousness, and to love that power by which they felt themselves redeemed. Thus, as the apostle says, "These showed the work of the law written in their hearts," and "did the things contained in the law," and so were no doubt justified and saved by the power of Christ in them. And as this was the judgment of the apostle, so it was also the belief of the primitive Christians. Hence Justin Martyr did not hesitate to call Socrates a Christian, saying that "all such as lived according to the divine Word in them, which was in all men, were Christians, such as Socrates and Heraclitus, and others among the Greeks."

Augustine says, "I do not think that the Jews dare affirm that none belonged to God but the Israelites."[66] And referring to these words, Ludovicus Vives says, "Thus the Gentiles, not having a law, were a law unto themselves; and the light of so living is the gift of God, and proceeds from the Son, of whom it is written that He enlightens every man that comes into the world."

Conclusion

Seeing then it is by this inward Gift, Grace, and Light, that both those who have the Gospel preached to them come to have Jesus brought forth in them, and to have the saving and sanctified use of all outward helps and advantages (i.e. Scriptures, teaching, etc.); and also, by this same Light, that God calls, invites, and strives with all, in a day of visitation, desiring the salvation of even those to whom He has withheld the outward knowledge of the gospel; we therefore, having experienced the inward and powerful work of this Light in our hearts—even Jesus Christ revealed in us—cannot cease to proclaim the Day of the Lord that has arisen within us, crying out with the woman of Samaria; "Come and see One that has told me all that ever I have done! Is not this the Christ?" This we do that others may come and experience the same thing in themselves, and may know that the little thing which reproves them in their hearts (however much they may have despised and neglected it), is nothing less than the Gospel

---

[66]   City of God, lib. 18, cap. 47

preached in them—"Christ, the wisdom and power of God," being in and by His Seed seeking to save their souls.

Of this Light therefore Augustine speaks in his Confessions: "In this beginning, O God, You made the heavens and the earth, in Your Word, in Your Son, in Your virtue, in Your wisdom, wonderfully saying, and wonderfully doing. Who shall comprehend it? Who shall declare it? What is that which shines in unto me, and smites my heart without hurt, at which I both tremble, and am inflamed? I tremble, in so far as I am unlike unto it; and I am inflamed in so far as I am made like unto it? It is Wisdom, which shines in unto me and dispels my cloud, which had again covered me, after I was departed from that darkness and heap of my punishments."[67] And again he says, "It is too late that I have loved You, O Beauty so old and so new; late have I loved You. And behold You were within, and I was without, and there I was seeking You! You did call, You did cry, You did break my deafness, You glanced, You did shine, You chased away my darkness."[68]

Of this our countryman, George Buchanan, also speaks as follows: "Truly I understand no other thing at present, than that Light which is divinely infused into our souls. For when God formed man, He not only gave him eyes for his body, by which he might shun those things that are hurtful to him, and follow those things that are profitable, but He has also set before his mind, as it were, a certain Light, by which he may discern things that are vile from things that are honest. Some call this power nature, others the law of nature; I truly judge it to be divine, and

---

[67]   lib. 11, cap. 9
[68]   lib. x., cap. 27

am persuaded that nature and wisdom never say different things. Moreover, in this God has given us a summary of the law, which in few words comprehends the whole, namely: that we should love Him from our hearts, and our neighbors as ourselves. And all the books of the Holy Scriptures which pertain to the forming of conduct, contain no more than a further explanation of this one law."[69]

This is that universal, evangelical Light, Grace, or Word in and by which the salvation of Christ is exhibited to all men, both Jew and Gentile, Scythian and Barbarian, of whatsoever country or kindred he may be. And therefore God has raised up unto Himself, in this our age, faithful witnesses and evangelists to preach again His everlasting Gospel, and to direct all—from the lofty professors of Christianity, who boast of the Law and the Scriptures and their outward knowledge of Christ, to the infidels and heathens that know Him not that way—that they may all come to mind the Light in them, and know Christ in them, whom James calls "the Just One [*ton Dikaion*], whom they have so long killed;"[70] that these may give up their sins, iniquities, false faith, professions, and outward righteousness, to be crucified by the power of His cross in them, and so know Christ within to be the "hope of glory," and may come to walk in His Light and be saved, who is that "true Light which gives light to every man coming into the world."

---

[69] De Jure Regni apud Scotos

[70] James 5:6

Chapter V.

Concerning Justification

The doctrine of justification comes next in order after discussing the extent of Christ's death and the grace thereby communicated. Many are the disputes among those called Christians concerning justification; but surely, if all were truly minding that power which justifies, there would be less noise about the various notions and opinions. I shall briefly review the controversy as it stands among others, and as I have often seriously observed it; and then state the controversy as it relates to us, opening our sense and judgment of it. Lastly, I will prove it (if the Lord permits) by some Scripture testimonies, and the certain experience of all who ever were truly justified.

That the doctrine of justification has been greatly corrupted by the church of Rome is not, I suppose, denied by any Protestant Christian, for it manifestly appears, and is openly taught among Catholics, that they obtain remission of sins, and justification by the merits of Christ, as these are applied to them in the use of the sacraments of the church, and are dispensed in the performance of various ceremonies, pilgrimages, indulgences, prayers, penances, and other performances, even though there be no inward renewing of the mind, or knowing of Christ inwardly formed; so that their justification comes from something outside of them, and not from Someone within them. These are said to be forgiven and made righteous by virtue of the sacrament itself, and by the authority of a priest who pronounces them absolved. Truly, Luther had great reason to oppose them on this matter, and if he had not run himself into another extreme (of which we will speak hereafter) his work would have stood the better. For in this, as in most other things, he is more to be commended for what he pulled down of Babylon than for what he built of his own.

The Protestants say that "they obtain remission of sins, and stand justified in the sight of God by virtue of the merits and sufferings of Christ, not by any infusing of His righteousness into them, but by the pardoning of their sins, and by accounting and accepting their persons as righteous; not for anything wrought in them, or done by them, but by imputing the obedience and satisfaction of Christ unto them by faith; which faith they have not of themselves, it is the gift of God."[1]

So then, we see that the justification of both Catholics and Protestants is not placed in any inward renewing of the mind, or by virtue of any spiritual birth or formation of Christ within them, but only by a bare application of His death and sufferings outwardly performed for them. The one lays hold of a faith given to them, and hopes to be justified by it alone; the other expects to make the death of Christ effectual unto them by the performance of some outward prayers and ceremonies. I admit, however (being

---

[1]   So says the Westminster Confession of Faith, chap. 11, sect. 1.

unwilling to wrong any), that some better things have been said as to the necessity of inward holiness, both by some modern Catholics and modern Protestants, who have come near to the Truth (as will hereafter appear, by some citations from their writings).

Our Position

As to our position on this matter: First, we renounce the idea of there being any natural power or ability in ourselves to bring us out of our lost and fallen condition and first nature; and confess that, as of ourselves, we are able to do nothing that is good. We further say that we are entirely unable to procure remission of sins or justification by any act of our own so as to merit it or draw it as a debt from God due unto us. Instead, we acknowledge all to be of and from His love, which is the origin and fundamental cause of our acceptance.

Secondly, God manifested this love towards us in the sending of His beloved Son, the Lord Jesus Christ, into the world, who gave Himself for us as an offering and a sacrifice to God, for a sweet-smelling savor, making peace through the blood of His cross, that He might reconcile us unto Himself. This One, by the Eternal Spirit, offered Himself without spot unto God, and suffered for our sins, the just for the unjust, that He might bring us unto God.

Thirdly then, forasmuch as all men (who have come to a man's state) have sinned—the Man Jesus only excepted—therefore all have need of this Savior, to remove the wrath of God from them, due to their offenses. In this respect, He is truly said to have "borne the iniquities of us all in His body on the tree,"[2] and is therefore the only Mediator, having qualified the wrath of God towards us, so that our former sins stand not in our way, being, by virtue of His most satisfactory sacrifice, removed and pardoned. And indeed, remission of sins is not to be expected, sought, or obtained in any other way, or by any works or sacrifice whatsoever (though, as has been said formerly, some may come to partake of this remission that are ignorant of the history).

So then Christ, by His death and sufferings has reconciled us to God, even while we are enemies—that is, He offers reconciliation unto the world, we are put into a capacity of being reconciled, God is willing to forgive us our iniquities and to accept us, as is well expressed by the apostle: "God was in Christ, reconciling the world unto Himself, not imputing their trespasses to them, and has put in us the Word of reconciliation."[3] And therefore the apostle, in the very next verses, entreats them "in Christ's stead to be reconciled to God;" intimating, that the wrath of God has been removed by the obedience of Christ Jesus, and now God is willing to be reconciled unto them, and is ready to remit the sins that are past, if they repent.

We therefore consider our redemption in a two-fold respect or state, both of which in their own nature are perfect, though in their application to us the one cannot be without respect to the other, as will be seen.

The first then, is the redemption performed and accomplished by Christ *for us* in His crucified body with-

---

[2]   1 Peter 2:24

[3]   2 Corinthians 5:19 Literal Translation. Editor's Note: Most modern translations read "has committed to us the word or message of reconciliation." But the Greek reads "placing in us the word of reconciliation" - θέμενος ἐν ἡμῖν τὸν λόγον τῆς καταλλαγῆς

out us. The other is the redemption wrought by Christ *within us*, which is no less properly called and accounted a redemption than the former. The first is that whereby man, as he stands in the fall, is put into a capacity of salvation, and has conveyed unto him a measure of that power, virtue, spirit, life, and grace that was in Christ Jesus—which, as the free gift of God, is able to overcome and root out the evil seed with which we are naturally leavened in the fall. The second is that whereby we experience and know this pure and perfect redemption in ourselves, purifying, cleansing, and redeeming us from the power of corruption, and bringing us into unity, favor, and friendship with God.[4]

By the first of these two, we, who were lost in Adam, plunged into the bitter and corrupt seed, unable, of ourselves to do any good thing, but naturally joined and united to evil, forward and prone to all iniquity, servants and slaves of the power and spirit of darkness, are, notwithstanding all this, so far reconciled to God by the death of His Son, even while enemies, that we are put into a capacity of salvation, having the glad tidings of the Gospel of peace offered unto us, that God is reconciled unto us in Christ, and so calls and invites us to Himself. It is in this respect that we understand the following scriptures: "He put to death the enmity in Himself;"[5] "He loved us first,"[6]

---

4   Editor's Note: See also Ephesians chapter 1, where Paul first writes (vs. 7), "In Him <u>we have redemption</u> through His blood, the forgiveness of sins, according to the riches of His grace;" and then (vs. 14) declares the Holy Spirit to be the "guarantee of our inheritance <u>until the redemption</u> of the purchased possession."

5   Ephesians 2:14-15

6   1 John 4:19

"Seeing us in our blood, He said unto us, Live;"[7] "He Himself bore our sins in His own body on the tree;"[8] and "Christ also suffered once for sins, the just for the unjust;"[9] etc.

By the second, we experience this capacity brought into act, whereby receiving and not resisting the purchase of His death (namely, the Light, Spirit, and Grace of Christ revealed in us), we witness and possess a real, true and inward redemption from the power and prevalence of sin, and so come to be truly and really redeemed, justified, and made righteous, and to an experiential union and friendship with God. Thus He "gave Himself for us, that He might redeem us from all iniquity and purify for Himself His own special people;"[10] and thus we "know Him and the power of His resurrection, and the fellowship of His sufferings, being conformed to His death." This last follows the first in order, and is a consequence of it, proceeding from it, as an effect proceeds from its cause. So then, even as none can enjoy the last without the first having been established (such being the will of God); so also none can truly partake of the first, except as he experiences the last. Thus to us, they are both causes of our justification.

Now, by justification we do not understand merely the production of good works, even those works wrought by the Spirit of Christ; for these (as Protestants rightly affirm) are more an effect of justification, than the cause of it. Instead, we understanding this justification to be the for-

---

7   Ezekiel 16:6

8   1 Peter 2:24

9   1 Peter 3:18

10   Titus 2:14

mation of Christ in us, Christ born and brought forth in us, from which good works naturally proceed, even as fruit from a fruitful tree. It is this inward birth in us, bringing forth righteousness and holiness in us, that does justify us, which, having removed and done away the contrary nature and spirit that did bear rule and bring condemnation, is now in dominion over all in our hearts. Those then, that come to know Christ thus formed in them, do enjoy Him wholly and undividedly, who is "the Lord our righteousness."[11] This is what it means to be clothed with Christ, and to have put Him on, and such as these God truly accounts to be righteous and just.

This is far from the doctrine of Catholics, for the formal cause of justification is not the works (they being but an effect of it), but rather an inward birth, Jesus Christ brought forth in the heart, who is the well-beloved, whom the Father cannot but accept, together with all those who are thus sprinkled with the blood of Jesus and truly washed with it. And by this (i.e. Christ inwardly put on) also comes the communication of the goods of Christ unto us, "by which we come to be made partakers of the divine nature,"[12] as Peter says, and are made one with Him, as the branches with the vine, and so have a title and right to what He has done and suffered for us. In this way His obedience becomes ours, His righteousness ours, His death and sufferings ours. And by this nearness we often come to have a sense of His sufferings, and do suffer with His Seed that yet lies pressed and crucified in the hearts of the ungodly. So we travail with it, and for its redemption, and

---

[11]   Jeremiah 23:6

[12]   2 Peter 1:4

for the repentance of those souls that are yet crucifying the Lord of Glory—even as the apostle Paul, who by his sufferings is said to "fill up that which is behind of the afflictions of Christ for His body, which is the church,"[13] though this be a mystery sealed up from all the wise men that are yet ignorant of this Seed in themselves, and oppose it.

Finally, though we place remission of sins in the righteousness and obedience of Christ performed by Him in the flesh (as the procuring cause), and we hold ourselves truly justified by Christ Jesus formed and brought forth in us; yet we cannot (as some Protestants have unwarily done) exclude works from justification. For though, to speak properly, we are not justified *by* them, yet are we justified *in* them, and so they are necessary. The denying of this is not only contrary to Scripture's testimony, but has brought a great scandal to the Protestant religion, opened the mouths of accusers, and made many to feel falsely secure in a justification without good works. Moreover, though it is not safe to say good works are meritorious, yet the Scriptures plainly show that they are rewarded, so that many of those called Church Fathers have not been afraid to use the word "merit" in a qualified sense (though not as the Catholics do). However, not only do most Protestants deny them to be necessary, but they are sometimes not ashamed to call them hurtful, often saying that the best works, even of the saints, are defiled and polluted. Now, though we judge this to be true of the best works performed *by man,* endeavoring a conformity to the outward law by his own strength, and in his own will, yet we believe that such works as naturally proceed from this spiritual birth, and

---

13   Colossians 1:24

from the formation of Christ in us, are pure and holy, even as the root from which they come is pure. For this reason God accepts them, justifies us in them, and rewards us for them, of His own free grace.

The Proof of Our Position

The state of the controversy being thus described, these following positions must now be proved:

First: that the obedience, sufferings, and death of Christ is that by which the soul obtains remission of sins, and is the procuring cause of that grace by whose inward workings Christ comes to be formed inwardly, and the soul made conformable to Him, and so made just and justified. And therefore, it is with respect to this capacity and the offer of grace that God is said to be "reconciled" to us—though not in the sense that He is actually united to, or does actually account anyone just or justified, while they remain in their sins, continuing impure and unjust.

Secondly: that it is by this inward birth of Christ in man that we are made just, and therefore so accounted by God. So then, to speak plainly, it is not till Christ be brought forth in us that we are truly justified in the sight of God; for the term justification is used, both more properly and more frequently in Scripture, according to its proper meaning, which is "to make one just," and not merely to repute one so.

Thirdly: that since good works naturally flow from this

birth (as heat from a fire), they are therefore an absolute necessity to justification—not as the cause thereof, but as that in which we are justified, and without which we cannot be justified. And though these good works are not meritorious, nor draw any debt upon God, yet He cannot but accept and reward them, for it is contrary to His nature to deny His own, especially since these may be perfect in their kind, as proceeding from a pure and holy birth and root. It is therefore false and contrary to the Truth to suggest that the holiest works of the saints are defiled and sinful in the sight of God; for the good works which flow from the spiritual birth are not the works of the law which the apostle excluded from justification.

As to the first position, I first prove it from Romans 3:25: "Whom God has set forth to be a propitiation through faith in His blood, to declare His righteousness for the remission of sins that are past, through the forbearance of God." Here the apostle holds forth the extent and efficacy of Christ's death, showing that by it, and by faith in it, remission of sins that are past is obtained; and that in this the forbearance of God is exercised towards mankind. So that though men, for the sins they daily commit, deserve eternal death, yet, by virtue of that most satisfactory sacrifice of Christ Jesus, the grace and seed of God moves in love towards them during the day of their visitation to redeem man out of evil.

Secondly, if God were perfectly reconciled with men, and did esteem them just while they are actually unjust and continue in their sins, then He would have no controversy with them. But why is it then, throughout the whole of Scripture, that He so often complains and reasons with those who our opponents claim to be justified, telling them "that their iniquities have made a separation between them and their God."[14] For where there is a perfect and full reconciliation there is no separation. But to suggest that men may be fully reconciled to God even while they continue in their sins necessarily implies that sin makes not the least separation from God, and that man is justified *in his sins.* And from this would follow the most abominable consequence, that good works and great sins are alike in the sight of God, seeing that neither one serves to justify, nor to break reconciliation with God—which doctrine opens a door to false security and every lewd practice.

Thirdly, this would make void the whole practical doctrine of the Gospel, and make entirely unnecessary such things as faith, repentance, obedience, and the other conditions which are required to be performed[15] on our part. And certainly, these conditions are of a nature that they cannot be performed at one time only, but are to be done all of one's lifetime. But if we are already perfectly reconciled and justified before these conditions are performed, then they cannot be said to be needful, which is contrary to the express testimony of Scripture acknowledged by all Christians. For we read: "Without faith it is impossible to please God."[16] And, "For if you live according to the flesh you will die; but if by the Spirit you put to death the deeds of the body, you will live."[17] And to those who were con-

---

[14]   Isaiah 59:2

[15]   Editor's Note: These are performed in the grace that flows to us in the covenant, as is previously mentioned.

[16]   Hebrews 11:6

[17]   Romans 8:13

verted, the Lord said, "I will remove your candlestick from you, unless you repent,"[18] and Paul exclaimed, "You ran well. Who has hindered you from obeying the truth?" Were I to mention all the Scriptures that positively and evidently prove this, I might transcribe much of all the doctrinal part of the Bible. For Christ said "It is finished,"[19] and indeed did finish His work more than sixteen hundred years ago, offering His body a sacrifice for sin, opening a door of mercy to all, and communicating a measure of His grace by which all may see their sins, be able to repent, and thus experience redemption, reconciliation, and justification inwardly wrought by Him now. But if in saying "It is finished," He is understood to have so perfected and finished the redemption of man, and fully reconciled all that will be saved (either before they believe, as some say, or after they confess to the truth of the history of Christ, or are sprinkled with water, etc.), even though they continue in their sins, then the whole doctrinal part of the Bible is useless and of no profit. In vain were the apostles sent forth to preach the gospel; in vain does Scripture warn us not to drift away, nor nullify the grace of God, nor lose our first love, nor allow our hearts to be hardened and so come short of our rest, etc., and in vain do all Christian preachers bestow their labor, spend their lungs, and give forth writings, only to do that which is already perfectly done without them.

But lastly, this doctrine also makes void the present intercession of Christ for men. For what shall become of that great article of faith by which we affirm, "That He sits

---

[18] Revelation 2:5

[19] John 19:30

at the right hand of God daily making intercession for us?"[20] And for what end does "the Spirit Himself make intercession for us with groanings which cannot be uttered?"[21] For to make intercession for those who are not in a possibility of salvation is absurd. And to pray for those that are already reconciled, and perfectly justified, is to no purpose. Truly, I see no real solving of this, except by acknowledging the truth of the matter, namely: that Christ by His death removed the wrath of God, so far as to obtain remission of sins for as many as receive the Grace and Light that He communicates unto them, and has purchased for them by His blood. As they believe in this, they come to know remission of sins past, and power to save them from the dominion of sin, for "to as many as receive Him, He gives power to become the sons of God." These also know His power to wipe away any present sin into which they may fall by unwatchfulness or weakness, if, applying themselves to this grace, they truly repent. So then, none are sons, none are justified, none are reconciled, until they receive Christ in that little Seed in their hearts; and thus life eternal is offered to those, "who by patient continuance in well-doing, seek for glory, honor, and immortality." For, according to the prophet, "if the righteous man turns away from his righteousness, his righteousness shall be remembered no more."[22] Accordingly, none remain sons of God, nor are justified in the sight of God, unless they patiently continue in righteousness and well-doing. And therefore Christ lives always to

---

[20] Romans 8:34

[21] Romans 8:26-27

[22] Ezekiel 18:24

make intercession during the day of every man's visitation, that they may be converted. And when they are in some measure grown up in the life, He makes intercession that they may continue, and go on, and not faint, nor go back again. Much more might be said to confirm this truth; but I go on to take notice of the common objections against it.

Objections and Responses

Objection: The first and chief objection is drawn from that saying of the apostle (before mentioned): "God has reconciled us to himself by Jesus Christ: God was in Christ reconciling the world unto himself, not imputing their trespasses unto them."[23] From here it is inferred that Christ fully perfected the work of reconciliation while He was on earth.

Answer: If by "reconciliation" is understood the removing of wrath, and the purchase of that Grace by which we may come to be fully reconciled and united to God, then we agree to it. But that this verse speaks of no more than this appears from the verse itself; for when the apostle speaks in the perfect tense, saying, "He has reconciled us," he speaks of himself and the saints, who, having received the Grace of God purchased by Christ, were through faith in Him actually reconciled. But with regard to others, he speaks of the "Word of reconciliation" which was "put in them;"[24] and in the following verse says, "Now then, we are

---

[23]   2 Corinthians 5:18-19

[24]   2 Corinthians 5:19 Literal Translation. Editor's Note: Most modern translations read "has committed to us the word or message

ambassadors for Christ, as though God were pleading through us: we implore you on Christ's behalf, be reconciled to God."[25] Now if their reconciliation had already been perfectly accomplished, what need would there be for any entreating them to be reconciled? Ambassadors are not sent after peace is already perfected and reconciliation made, but to entreat for reconciliation.

Objection: Secondly, they object (from v. 21 of the same chapter), "For He made Him who knew no sin to be sin for us, that we might become the righteousness of God in Him." From this they argue, that as our sin is imputed to Christ, who had no sin; so Christ's righteousness is imputed to us, without our actually being righteous.

Answer: But this interpretation is easily rejected; for the apostle himself, in multiple instances, demonstrates that we are to be made *really* righteous by Christ, and not merely imputed or considered righteous. Indeed, this appears by what follows in verses 14-16 of the following chapter, where he argues largely against any supposed agreement between light and darkness, or righteousness and unrighteousness. But if men are to be reckoned engrafted in Christ, and real members of Him, merely by an external imputative righteousness, while they themselves continue in unrighteousness, would this not imply a fellowship between righteousness and unrighteousness? And truly, it should be considered strange how so many made this "imputed righteousness" so fundamental an arti-

---

of reconciliation." But the Greek reads "placing in us the word of reconciliation" - θέμενος ἐν ἡμῖν τὸν λόγον τῆς καταλλαγῆς

[25] 2 Corinthians 5:20

cle of their faith, though it is so contrary to the whole strain of the Gospel. For Christ did not, in any of His sermons and gracious speeches, ever desire His hearers to rely upon such a thing, but instead always pointed them to true sanctification, to the cleaning of the inside and outside of the cup, and to good works that glorify the Father, saying, "You shall be perfect, just as your Father in heaven is perfect."[26]

True Justification—Christ Formed Within

I come then to the second thing proposed by me, which is, that it is by this inward birth, or Christ formed within, that we are formally (so to speak) justified in the sight of God. I suppose I have said enough already to demonstrate how much we acknowledge the death and sufferings of Christ as that offering by which satisfaction is made to the justice of God, remission of sins is obtained, and the Grace and Seed are purchased, from which this birth proceeds. The thing which remains to be proved is, that by Christ Jesus formed in us we are justified, or *truly made just*. Let it be noted that I here use the term "justification" in this sense.

First then, I prove this by that Scripture of the apostle Paul, 1 Corinthians 6:11: "And such were some of you. But you were washed, but you were sanctified, but you were justified in the name of the Lord Jesus and by the Spirit of our God." The word "justified" here must necessarily signify a being made really just, and not being merely imputed such; or else "sanctified" and "washed" might also

---

[26]   Matthew 5:48

be considered a mere imputation, which overturns the whole intent of the context. For in the preceding verses, the apostle warns his readers "not to be deceived," for "the unrighteous cannot inherit the kingdom of God;" and after specifying several sorts of wickedness, concludes by saying "such were some of you" but you are so no longer. Thus having been washed and sanctified, so they were truly justified. For my part, I neither see anything, nor have ever heard or read anything, that could suggest the word "justified" in this place to be understood in any other way than in its own proper and genuine meaning of *being made just*.

Now this word "justify," which is derived from the noun "justice," or the adjective "just," does beyond all question signify a making just, for it is nothing other than a composition of the verb *facio*, and the adjective *justus*, which is *justifico*, or *I make just*. Likewise, the word justified is from *justus* and *fio*, meaning *I become just*. So it is with other verbs of this kind, like *santifico* which is from *sanctus* (holy) and *facio*, meaning *I make holy*. In each case it is understood that the subject is really and truly endued with that virtue and quality from which the verb is derived. For as none are said to be sanctified who are not really holy; so neither can any be truly said to be justified, while they actually remain unjust.

However, this verb "justify" has, in a metaphorical and figurative way, been used in a legal sense, as when a man really guilty of a crime is freed from the punishment of his sin, he is said to be justified, that is, put in the place as if he were just. But is it not strange that men should be so superficial in a matter of so great importance as to build the stress of their acceptance with God upon a mere borrowed and metaphorical meaning of this word, to the excluding (or at least esteeming unnecessary) that holiness without which Scripture expressly says, "No man shall ever see God?"[27] Indeed, would it not be a great mistake to content ourselves with an imaginary justification while God requires a real one? And let it be considered that in all the letters to the Romans, Corinthians, Galatians, and elsewhere, where the apostle handles this theme, the word may be taken in its own proper signification without any absurdity. For instance, in his epistles to the Romans and Galatians, Paul asserts that "a man cannot be justified by the law of Moses, nor by the works of the law."[28] There is no absurdity or danger in understanding it here according to its own proper meaning, namely, that a man cannot be made just by the law of Moses, especially seeing how this so well agrees with that saying of the same apostle, That "the law makes nothing perfect."[29] Also where it is said, "We are justified by faith,"[30] it may be very well understood of being made just, seeing it is also said that "faith purifies the heart;"[31] and no doubt the pure in heart are just, and "the just live by faith."[32] Again, where it is said, "We are justified by grace,"[33] or "We are justified by Christ,"[34] or "We are justified by the Spirit;"[35] it is in no way absurd to

---

[27] Hebrews 12:14

[28] Romans 3:28; Galatians 2:16, 3:11

[29] Hebrews 7:19

[30] Romans 3:28; Galatians 3:24

[31] Acts 15:9

[32] Habakkuk 2:4; Romans 1:17; Galatians 3:11; Hebrews 10:38

[33] Romans 3:24; Titus 3:7

[34] Galatians 2:17

[35] 1 Corinthians 6:11

understand it as being made just, seeing that by His Spirit and grace He does indeed make men just. But to understand it universally the other way, as a mere legal acceptance, would infer great absurdities, as might be proved at large, but because I judged it would be acknowledged, I forbear at present, for brevity's sake.

But further, in the most weighty places where this word "justify" is used in Scripture, our adversaries must acknowledge it to be understood as making just, and not as a bare legal acceptation. This we have seen in 1 Corinthians 6:11, "But you were washed, but you were sanctified, but you were justified." But also in Titus 3:5-7—"According to His mercy He saved us, through the washing of regeneration and renewing of the Holy Spirit, whom He poured out on us abundantly through Jesus Christ our Savior, that having been justified by His grace we should become heirs according to the hope of eternal life." And also in that excellent saying of the apostle (Romans 8:30), "Whom He called, these He also justified; and whom He justified, these He also glorified." This is commonly called the "golden chain," and is acknowledged by all to comprehend the method and order of salvation. But if "justified" were not here understood in its proper signification—of actually being made just—then a true change from wickedness to holiness would be wholly excluded from this chain. But surely (as most do acknowledge), the apostle, in this abbreviated account, uses the word "justified" to comprehend all that comes between calling and glorifying, insinuating that being made really righteous is the means by which we pass from calling to glorification.

Indeed many Church Fathers and famous Protestants

do acknowledge the same: "I take," says Beza, "the name of justification generally, as comprehending whatsoever we acquire from Christ, whether by imputation, or by the efficacy of the Spirit in sanctifying us. So likewise should the word justification be taken in Romans 8:30."[36] Melanchthon says, "That to be justified by faith, signifies in Scripture not only to be pronounced just, but also, from unrighteous to be made righteous."[37] Also, some chief Protestants, though not so clearly, have hinted at our doctrine, whereby we ascribe unto the death of Christ remission of sins, and the work of justification unto the grace of the Spirit acquired by His death. Martin Borrhaus, explaining Romans 4:25 where it says, "Who was given for our sins, and rose again for our justification," says: "There are two things here beheld in Christ, which are necessary to our justification;—the one is His death; the other is His arising from the dead. By His death, the sins of this world were expiated. By His rising from the dead, it pleased the same goodness of God to give the Holy Spirit, whereby both the Gospel is believed, and the righteousness which was lost by the fault of the first Adam, is restored."[38] And afterwards he says, "The apostle expresses both parts in these words, 'Who was given for our sins, and rose again for our justification.' In His death is beheld the satisfaction for sin; in His resurrection is beheld the gift of the Holy Spirit, by which our justification is perfected."[39] And William Forbes, bishop of Edinburgh, says, "Whensoever the Scripture

---

[36]   In cap. 3. ad Tit. ver. 7.
[37]   In Apol. Confess. Aug.
[38]   In Gen. cap. 15. ad verb. Cred dit Abraham Deo., p. 161.
[39]   lib. 3. Reg. cap. 9. ver. 4., p. 681.

makes mention of the justification before God, it appears that the word justify necessarily signifies not only to pronounce just, in a legal sense, but also really and inherently to make just; for God justifies differently than earthly judges. Indeed, both the Scriptures and the Fathers do affirm, that in the justification of a sinner, their sins are not only remitted, forgiven, covered, and not imputed, but also taken away, blotted out, cleansed, washed, purged, and very far removed from us, as appears from many places of the holy Scriptures."[40]

The Revelation of Jesus Christ in the Soul

Having then sufficiently shown that by "justification" we should understand a really being made righteous, I now do boldly affirm (not only from a notional knowledge, but from a real, inward, experiential feeling of the thing), that the immediate, nearest, or formal cause of a man's justification in the sight of God, is the revelation of Jesus Christ in the soul, changing, altering, and renewing the mind. It is by Him (the Author of this inward work), thus revealed and formed within, that we are truly justified and accepted in the sight of God. For it is as we are covered and clothed with Him in whom the Father is always well pleased, that we may draw near to God, and stand with confidence before His throne, being purged by the blood of Jesus inwardly poured into our souls, and clothed with His life and righteousness therein revealed. And this is that order and method of salvation held forth by the apostle in that divine saying (Romans 5:10): "For if, when we were ene-

---

[40]   In considerat. modest. de Just. lib. 2. Sect. 8.

mies, we were reconciled to God by the death of His Son, much more being reconciled, we shall be saved by His life." Here the apostle first holds forth reconciliation wrought by the death of Christ (wherein God is near to receive and redeem man), and then man's salvation and real justification wrought by the life of Jesus. Now this life is an inward, spiritual thing revealed in the soul, whereby the soul is renewed and brought forth out of death (where it naturally has been by the fall), and so quickened and made alive unto God.

Of this saving life the apostles speak frequently, commending all disciples to the inward working of its power. Paul, upon taking leave of the Ephesians, says, "So now, brethren, I commend you to God and to the Word of His grace, which is able to build you up and give you an inheritance among all those who are sanctified."[41] And in his letter to the same, he speaks of "the exceeding greatness of His power toward us who believe." James directs his readers to "the implanted word, which is able to save your souls."[42] Elsewhere, Paul writes, "Even when we were dead in trespasses, He made us alive together with Christ (by grace you have been saved), and raised us up together."[43] Now, this "making alive" and "raising together" doubtless speaks of the inward work of renovation; therefore the apostle here mentions their being saved by grace, which is the inward virtue and power of Christ in the soul. Of this the apostle also speaks in 2 Corinthians 4:10: "That the life also of Jesus might be made manifest in our body;" and

---

[41]   Acts 20:32

[42]   James 1:21

[43]   Ephesians 2:5-6

verse 11: "That the life of Jesus also might be made manifest in our mortal flesh." And it is by this inward life of Jesus Christ revealed and formed (as before observed) that "we are saved."

Furthermore, the truth of our being justified by this revelation of Jesus Christ, and the new creation brought forth in us, does evidently appear from that excellent saying of the apostle in Titus 3:5: "According to His mercy He saved us, through the washing of regeneration and renewing of the Holy Spirit, whom He poured out on us abundantly through Jesus Christ our Savior, that having been justified by His grace we should become heirs according to the hope of eternal life." So then, that which saves us is evidently also that which justifies us, these words being more or less synonymous in this respect. Here the apostle clearly ascribes the immediate cause of justification to this inward work of regeneration, which is Jesus Christ revealed and formed in the soul; for this washing of regeneration is no doubt that inward power and virtue whereby the soul is cleansed and clothed with the righteousness of Christ, so as to be made fit to appear before God.

This doctrine is also manifest from 2 Corinthians 13:5 —"Examine yourselves as to whether you are in the faith. Test yourselves. Do you not know yourselves, that Jesus Christ is in you?—unless indeed you are reprobates." First, it appears here how earnest the apostle was that they should know Christ to be in them, for he presses this exhortation upon them three times. Secondly, he makes the cause of reprobation (or of non-justification) the lack of Christ thus revealed and known in the soul. Thus it necessarily follows, that wherever Christ is inwardly known, there the persons subjected to Him are approved and justified. Nothing could be more plain than this; for if we must know Christ in us, except we be reprobates (or unjustified persons), then those who *do* know Him in them are *not* reprobates, and consequently justified persons. For this reason, the same apostle says: "My little children, for whom I travail in birth again until Christ be formed in you,"[44] also using this language—"Christ within, the hope of glory."[45]

Now, in insisting upon this inward work, we are far from denying that the origin and fundamental cause of our justification is the love of God manifested in the appearance of Jesus Christ in the flesh, who by His life, death, sufferings and obedience, made a way for our reconciliation, becoming a sacrifice for the remission of sins that are past. Yet, "through one Man's righteous act the free gift came to all men,"[46] for He purchased unto us His Seed and Grace from which this inward birth arises, and in which Jesus Christ is inwardly received, formed, and brought forth in us, in His own pure and holy image of righteousness. By this alone our souls live unto God, and are clothed with Him, and have put Him on, even as the Scripture speaks (Eph. 4:23-24; Gal. 3:27). We stand justified and saved in and by Him, and by His Spirit and grace (Rom. 3:24; 1 Cor. 6:11; Tit. 3:7). Hereby we are made partakers of the fullness of His merits, and indeed, His cleansing blood is near to wash away every sin and weakness, and to heal all our backslidings as often as we turn towards Him

---

44   Galatians 4:19
45   Colossians 1:27-28
46   Romans 5:18

by unfeigned repentance to become renewed by His Spirit.

Therefore, those who find Christ thus raised and ruling in them have a true ground of hope to believe that they are justified by His blood. But let not any deceive themselves, so as to encourage themselves in a vain hope or confidence that by the death and sufferings of Christ they are justified, even while "sin lies at their door,"[47] iniquity prevails, and they remain yet unrenewed and unregenerate —lest it be said unto them at last, "I never knew you; depart from Me."[48] Let that saying of Christ be remembered, "Not everyone who says to Me, 'Lord, Lord,' shall enter the kingdom of heaven, but he who does the will of My Father in heaven."[49] And with this consider those excellent sayings of the beloved disciple: "Little children, let no one deceive you. He who practices righteousness is righteous, just as He is righteous. He who sins is of the devil."[50] And "if our heart condemns us, God is greater than our heart, and knows all things."[51]

Many famous Protestants bear witness to this justification by Christ inwardly revealed and formed in man. Martin Borrhaus says, "The form of our justification is the divine righteousness itself, by which we are made just and good. This is Jesus Christ, who is called 'our righteousness,' partly from the forgiveness of sins, and partly from the renewing and the restoring of that integrity which was lost by the fault of the first Adam, so that the new and

---

[47]   Genesis 4:7

[48]   Matthew 7:23

[49]   Matthew 7:21

[50]   1 John 3:7-8

[51]   1 John 3:20

heavenly Adam is put on by us, of which the apostle says, 'You have put on Christ.'"[52] Zwingli also, says, "The sanctification of the Spirit is true justification, which alone suffices to justify."[53] Estius, commenting upon 1 Cor. 6:11, says, "Lest Christian righteousness should be thought to consist in the washing alone, that is, in the remission of sins, Paul adds the other degree or part, 'but you are sanctified;' that is, you have attained to purity, so that you are now truly holy before God. Lastly, expressing the sum of the benefit received in one word, which includes both the parts, the apostle adds, 'but you are justified in the name of the Lord Jesus Christ and by the Spirit of our God.'" And lastly, Richard Baxter, the famous English preacher, says, "Some ignorant wretches gnash their teeth at this doctrine, as if it were flat Roman Catholicism, not understanding the nature of the righteousness of the new covenant; which is all out of Christ in ourselves, though wrought by the power of the Spirit of Christ in us."[54]

The Necessity of Good Works

The third thing to be considered is concerning good works, which, as we have said, do naturally flow from this spiritual birth, as heat from a fire, and are therefore absolute necessity to justification—not as the cause thereof, but as that in which we are justified, and without which we cannot be justified.

I suppose enough has already been said to clear us

---

[52] *In Gen.* pag. 181

[53] In his epistle to the princes of Germany, as cited by Himelius, c. vii., p. 60,

[54] In his book called *Aphorisms of Justification*, p. 80

from any charges of being similar to the Roman Catholics in this matter. But if it be asked, whether will affirm that a man is justified by works? I answer—I hope none will take offense if in this matter we use the plain language of the Holy Scripture, which expressly says: (James 2:24) "You see then that a man is justified by works, and not by faith only." I need not offer to prove the truth of this saying, since what is said in this chapter by the apostle is sufficient to convince any man that will but read and believe it. I shall only derive this one argument:

Argument: If no man can be justified without faith, and no faith can be living or suitable to justification without works, then works are necessary to justification.

This truth is so apparent and evident in the Scriptures that, for the proof of it, we might transcribe most of the precepts of the Gospel. I shall instance a few which so clearly assert the thing in question that they need no commentary nor further demonstration, and then answer the common objections made against this. Hebrew 12:14, "Without holiness no man shall see God;" Matthew 7:21, "Not every one that says unto Me, Lord, Lord, shall enter into the kingdom of heaven, but he that does the will of my Father who is in heaven;" John 13:17, "If you know these things, happy are you if you do them;" 1 Corinthians 7:19, "Circumcision is nothing, and uncircumcision is nothing, but the keeping of the commandments of God;" Rev. 22:14, "Blessed are they that do His commandments, that they may have right to the tree of life and through the gates may enter into the city;" Indeed, many more might be given as examples, from all of which I argue:

Argument: If only those who do the will of the Father can enter the kingdom of heaven; if only those who do the sayings of Christ are accounted the wise and happy builders; if no outward observations avail, but only the keeping of the commandments; and if only those who do His commandments have right to the Tree of Life, and an entrance through the gates of the city; then works are absolutely necessary to salvation and justification.

Objection: But they object that works are not necessary to justification because of the saying of Christ in Luke 17:10: "When you have done all those things which you are commanded, say, 'We are unprofitable servants,'" etc.

Answer: As to God we are indeed unprofitable, for He needs nothing, and we can add nothing to Him. But as to ourselves we are not unprofitable, else it might be said that it is not profitable for a man to keep God's commandments, which is most absurd and would contradict Christ's doctrine throughout the Scriptures. Does not Christ pronounce those men "good and faithful servants" who improved their talents?[55] Was not their doing so profitable unto them? It is said of the one that hid his talent and did not improve it, "Cast the unprofitable servant into the outer darkness." If failing to improve the talent made this man unprofitable, then improving their talents indeed made the others profitable, especially seeing how Christ said of them, "Well done, good and faithful servant, you

---

[55]   Matthew 21:14-30

have been faithful over a few things, I will make you ruler over many things; enter into the joy of your Lord."[56]

Objection: Secondly, they object from those sayings of the apostle Paul, where he excludes the deeds of the law from justification: such as Romans 3:20, "Therefore by the deeds of the Law no flesh will be justified in His sight," and verse 28, "Therefore we conclude that a man is justified by faith apart from the deeds of the Law."

Answer: In answer to this objection, I say, there is a great difference between the works of the Law, and the works of grace or of the Gospel. The first are excluded, the second are not, but are necessary. The first are those which are performed in man's own will and by his strength, in a conformity to the outward law and letter, and therefore are man's own imperfect works, or the works of the Law which makes nothing perfect.[57] And to this kind belong all the ceremonies, purifications, washings, and traditions of the Jews. The second are the works of the Spirit of Grace in the heart, wrought in conformity to the inward and spiritual law. These works are not wrought in man's will, nor by his power and ability, but in and by the power and Spirit of Christ in us, and therefore are pure and perfect according to their kind. Indeed, these may be called Christ's works, for He is the immediate author and worker of them.[58] Such works we absolutely affirm to be necessary to justification, so that a man cannot be justified without them; for all faith

---

[56]   Matthew 21:23

[57]   Hebrews 7:19

[58]   See Hebrews 13:20-21; Philippians 1:11, 2:13

without them is dead and useless, as says the apostle James.

Now, that this distinction between works of the Law and works of grace is to be admitted, and that the apostle excludes the first from justification but not the second, clearly appears when we consider the context of these assertions. For in both his letter to the Romans and to the Galatians where he speaks to this purpose, we find that many of the Gentiles (who were not of the seed of Abraham according to the flesh) had been converted to the Christian faith, and come to believe in Him. Yet some among the Jewish converts to the faith sought to subject the believing Gentiles to the legal ceremonies and observations of the Law, insisting that these were necessary to their justification. This gave the apostle Paul occasion at length to show the use and tendency of the Law, and of its works, and to distinguish them from the faith of Christ and the righteousness thereof, showing that the former had ceased and become ineffectual, but the latter remained, and was necessary. And the kind of works excluded by the apostle is evident by the whole strain of his epistle to the Galatians. For in the fourth chapter, he reproves them for returning to the observation of days and times,[59] and in the fifth and sixth he shows them the folly of adhering to the ceremony of circumcision, saying: "For in Christ Jesus neither circumcision nor uncircumcision avails anything, but faith working through love;"[60] and "For in Christ Jesus neither circumcision nor uncircumcision avails anything, but a

---

[59]   Galatians 4:10-11
[60]   Galatians 5:6

new creation."[61] Now circumcision is a word which is often used to comprehend the whole of the old covenant, with its ceremonial and legal performances. These, Paul says, are excluded, and by them no man is justified; but faith work-ing through love, but the new creature, *this* is that which avails, and indeed is necessary. Now, that the apostle in no way intends to exclude the good works of the new creature appears in this same place, for he tells them plainly: "Do not be deceived, God is not mocked; for whatever a man sows, that he will also reap. For he who sows to his flesh will of the flesh reap corruption, but he who sows to the Spirit will of the Spirit reap everlasting life. And let us not grow weary while doing good, for in due season we shall reap if we do not lose heart." Does it not clearly appear by this how necessary these good works are—not the outward ceremonies and traditions of the Law, but the fruits of the Spirit mentioned a little before (4:22), by which Spirit Paul desired them all to be led, and in which he would have them all walk. The former are "works of righteousness that *we* have done," wrought in our first, fallen nature, by our own strength, in legal performances. The latter are the fruits of "the washing of regeneration, and the renewing of the Holy Spirit."[62]

Objection: But these works of the Spirit may also be called ours, because they are wrought in us, and also buy us many times as instruments.

Answer: Even so, the two kinds of works differ widely from each other. In the first we are yet alive in our own natural

---

[61] Galatians 6:15

[62] See Titus 3:5

state, unrenewed, working of ourselves, seeking to save ourselves by imitating and endeavoring a conformity to the outward letter of the Law, and so wrestling and striving in the carnal mind that is enmity to God, and in the cursed will which is not yet subdued. But in the second we are "crucified with Christ,"[63] having become "dead with Him,"[64] being partakers "of the fellowship of His sufferings," and made "conformable to His death."[65] Here our first man, our "old man with all his deeds"[66] (both the openly wicked and the seemingly righteous), are all buried and nailed to the cross of Christ, and so it is no more we but Christ alive in us—the Worker living in us. So then, though it be us in a sense, yet it is according to that sense of the apostle in Galatians 2:20, "I have been crucified with Christ; it is no longer I who live, but Christ lives in me;" or, "I labored more abundantly than they all, yet not I, but the grace of God which was with me."[67] These works are most certainly to be ascribed to the Spirit of Christ and the grace of God in us, as being immediately done, enabled, or led by Him. And this manner of speech is not at all strained, but was familiar to the apostles, as often appears in Scripture: such as Galatians 2:8: "For He who worked effectively in Peter for the apostleship to the circumcised also worked effectively in me toward the Gentiles;" or, "For it is God who works in you both to will and to do for His good pleasure," etc.

---

[63] Galatians 2:20
[64] Romans 6:3
[65] Philippians 3:10
[66] Colossians 3:9
[67] 1 Corinthians 15:10

Objection: Some object that no works, not even the works of Christ in us, can have place in justification, because nothing that is impure can be useful in it; and all the works wrought in us are impure. To prove this they allege that saying of the prophet Isaiah: "All our righteousness is as a filthy rag;"[68] adding this reason, that, seeing we are impure, so our works must be also; for even the works of God, as performed by us, receive a tincture of impurity, even as clean water passing through an unclean pipe is defiled.

Answer: That no impure works are useful to justification is confessed; but that all works wrought in the saints are impure is denied. And to answer this objection, the above-mentioned distinction between the two sorts of works will also serve us here. For we confess that the first sort of works are impure; but not the second—because the first sort is wrought by man in the unrenewed state, but the other is wrought by the Spirit and grace of God. And as for that place in Isaiah, it must relate to the first sort; for though he says, "All *our* righteousness is as a filthy rag," yet this does not comprehend the righteousness of Christ wrought in us, but only that which we work of and by ourselves. For were it otherwise, then it would follow that we should throw away all holiness and righteousness as a filthy rag,[69] even the fruits of the Spirit, mentioned in Galatians 5. But to the contrary, some of the works of the saints are said to have been a "sweet savor in the nostrils of the

---

[68]   Isaiah 64:6
[69]   Lit. "a menstrual garment"

Lord;"[70] and an "ornament of great price in the sight of God;"[71] which are said to "prevail with Him," and to be "acceptable to Him;"[72] which filthy rags cannot be (as many well-known Protestants have acknowledged).

As to the other part of this objection—that seeing the best of men are still impure and imperfect, therefore their works must be so—this involves a great assumption, one which we deny, as will be discussed at length in the next proposition. Yet even in the case of a man not thoroughly perfect in all respects, this will not preclude all good or perfect works (according to their kind) from being brought forth in him by the Spirit of Christ; neither does the example of water going through an unclean pipe hit the mark; because though water may be tinctured with uncleanness, yet the Spirit of God cannot, whom we assert to be the immediate Author of those works that avail in justification. Consequently, we say that Jesus Christ's works in His children are pure and perfect, and that He works in and through that pure thing of His own forming and creating in them.

Moreover, if our adversaries' supposition held true, then it would follow that the very miracles and works of the apostles, which Christ wrought in them, and which they wrought in and by the Power, Spirit, and Grace of Christ, were also impure and imperfect. And indeed, would not also the writing of the Holy Scriptures (which our adversaries seem so much to magnify) of necessity be impure and imperfect, as coming through impure and

---

[70] Philippians 4:18; 2 Corinthians 2:15

[71] 1 Peter 3:4

[72] See Romans 12:1-2, 14:18; Philippians 4:18; 1 Timothy 2:3, 5:4; 1 Peter 2:5, 2:30.

imperfect vessels?

But lastly, because it seems fit here to say something of the merit and reward of works, I shall add something in this place of our sense and belief concerning that matter. We are far from thinking or believing that man merits any-thing by his works from God, for indeed all is of free grace, and therefore we have always denied the Catholic notion of *meritum ex condigno.*[73] Nevertheless we cannot help but acknowledge, that God, out of His infinite goodness with which He has loved mankind, after He communicates to him His holy Grace and Spirit, does, according to His own will, recompense and reward the good works of His chil-dren. And therefore, a merit of reward, in the sense that the Scriptures plainly and positively assert it, we may not deny. For the same Greek word *axion*, which signifies "merit," is found in those places where the translators express it "worth," or "worthy," (as in Matt. 3:8; 1 Thess. 2:12; 2 Thess. 1:5, 11.)

Those who are called the Fathers of the church fre-quently used the word "merit" in this way, and many Protestants have shown themselves not opposed to this word in the sense that we use it. The Apology for the Augustan confession, art. 20, has these words: "We agree that works are truly meritorious, not of the remission of sins or justification; but they are meritorious of other rewards both natural and spiritual, which are indeed both in this life and after this life." G. Voss, in his theological thesis concerning the merits of good works, says; "We have

---

73 Editor's Note: *Meritum ex condigno*, is the Roman Catholic doc-trine stating that there is an intrinsic worth in works, which God, if He does according to justice, cannot but reward with eternal life.

not gone as far as to condemn the word 'merit' altogether, as being that which both many of the ancients use, and also the reformed churches have used in their confessions. Now, that God judges and accepts men according to their works is beyond doubt to any who will seriously read and consider the following scriptures: Matt. 16:27; Rom. 2:6-7,10; 2 Cor. 5:10; James 1:25; Heb. 10:36; 1 Pet. 1:17; Rev. 22:12."

Conclusion

To conclude this theme, let none be so bold as to mock God, supposing themselves justified and accepted in the sight of God by virtue of Christ's death and sufferings, while they remain unsanctified and unjustified in their own hearts, and polluted in their sins—lest their hope prove to be that of the hypocrite, which perishes.[74] And on the other hand, let none foolishly imagine that they can, by their own works, or by the performance of any ceremonies or traditions, or by the giving of money, or by afflicting their bodies in will worship and voluntary humility, or foolishly striving to conform themselves to the outward letter of the law, flatter themselves that they merit anything before God, or draw a debt upon Him. Indeed, let no one think that men have power to make such things effectual to their justification, lest they be found foolish boasters and strangers to Christ and His righteousness. But blessed forever are they who have truly had a sense of their own unworthiness and sinfulness, who have seen all their own endeavors and performances to be fruitless and vain. Yes,

---

[74] Job 8:13

blessed are they who have beheld their own emptiness, and the worthlessness of their vain hopes, faith, and confidence, while being inwardly pricked, pursued, and condemned by God's holy witness in their hearts. For these, having surrendered themselves to this inward witness, and allowed His grace to work in them, have become changed and renewed in the spirit of their minds, passed from death to life, and come to know Jesus arisen in them, working both the will and the deed. These have indeed "put on the Lord Jesus Christ,"[75] and are clothed with Him, and partake of His righteousness and nature, and so can draw near to the Lord with boldness, knowing their acceptance in and by Him in whom the Father is well pleased.

---

[75]   Romans 13:14

CHAPTER VI.

CONCERNING PERFECTION

Since we have placed justification in the experience of Jesus Christ revealed, formed, and brought forth in the heart—there working His works of righteousness and bringing forth the fruits of the Spirit—the question that now confronts us is how far He may prevail in us while we are in this life? Or how far may we prevail over our souls' enemies, in and by His strength?

Those that plead for a justification wholly without them, merely by an imputed righteousness, denying the necessity of being clothed with real and inward righteousness, do consequently affirm that it is "impossible" for a man, even "the best of men, to be free of sin in this life, which," they say, "no man ever was." On the contrary, they insist that none can, "neither of himself, nor by any grace received in this life [O, wicked saying against the power of God's Grace!], keep the commandments of God perfectly, but that every man does break the commandments in thought, word and deed."[1] From this they also affirm (as was observed before), that the very best actions of the saints, even their prayers and worship, are impure and polluted.

---

[1] These are the words of the Westminster larger Catechism.

Now, we freely acknowledge this to be true of the natural, fallen man, in his first state, whatever his profession or pretense may be, so long as he is unconverted and unregenerate. However, we do believe that, to those in whom Christ comes to be formed, and the new man brought forth and born of the incorruptible seed, as that birth (and the man in union with it) naturally does the will of God, so it is possible to keep to it in such a way as not to be found daily transgressors of the law of God. And for the more clear stating of the controversy, let the following be considered:

First, that we do not place this possibility in man's own will and capacity, as he is a man, the son of fallen Adam, or as he is in his natural state, however wise or knowing, or however much he is endued with a notional and literal knowledge of Christ, thereby endeavoring a conformity to the letter of the outward law.

Secondly, we attribute this wholly to man as he is born again, renewed in his mind, raised by Christ, knowing Christ alive, reigning and ruling in him, guiding and leading him by His Spirit, and revealing in him the law of the Spirit of life—which not only manifests and reproves sin, but also gives power to come out of it.

Thirdly, by this we do not intend such a perfection as does not allow for of a daily growth, and so do not mean we are to be as pure, holy, and perfect as God in His divine attributes of wisdom, knowledge and purity. Rather, we speak of a perfection proportionable and answerable to man's measure, whereby we are kept from transgressing the law of God and enabled to answer what He requires of us. Even as a little gold is perfect gold in its kind, as well as a great mass, and as a child has a perfect body as well as a man, though it daily grows more and more. Thus Christ is said (Luke 2:52) to have "increased in wisdom and stature, and in favor with God and man," though before that time He had never sinned, and was no doubt perfect, in a true and proper sense.

Fourthly, though a man may witness this for a season (and therefore all ought to press after it), nevertheless, those who have attained it in measure, may, by the wiles and temptations of the enemy, fall into iniquity, and lose it sometimes, if they are not watchful, and do not diligently attend to that Seed of God in the heart. And we do not doubt but that many good and holy men have had some ebbings and flowings of this kind, for though every sin weakens a man in his spiritual condition, yet it does not necessarily destroy him altogether, or render him incapable of rising again.

Lastly, though I affirm that after a man has arrived to such a sinless condition, he may yet fall and sin again, I will nevertheless not deny but there may be a state attainable in this life, in which to do righteousness may become so natural to the regenerate soul, that in the stability of this condition they cannot sin. Others may perhaps speak more certainly of this state, if they have arrived to it. With respect to myself, I shall speak modestly, as acknowledging myself not to have arrived at it. However, I dare not deny that there is such a state, for it seems so clearly to be asserted by the apostle in the following words, "Whoever has been born of God does not sin, for His seed remains in him; and he cannot sin, because he has been born of God."[2]

Having then stated the controversy, I shall proceed

---

[2] 1 John 3:9

first to show the absurdity of that doctrine that pleads for sin for term of life, even in the saints. Secondly, I will prove our doctrine of perfection from many clear testimonies of the holy Scriptures. And lastly, I will answer the arguments and objections of our opposers.

The Folly of Contending for Sin

First then, the doctrine which states that saints can never be free from sinning in this life, is inconsistent with the wisdom of God and with His glorious power and majesty, "who is of purer eyes than to behold evil, and cannot look upon wickedness;" for He who purposed in Himself to gather a people to worship Him in Spirit and truth, and to witness for Him on the earth, is doubtless able to sanctify and purify them. God has no delight in iniquity, but abhors transgression, and though He regards man in transgression so far as to pity him and afford him a means to come out of it, yet He has no delight in man as he remains in that state. For if man must always be joined to sin, then God should always be at a distance from them, as it is written (Isa. 59:2), "Your iniquities have separated you from your God, and your sins have hidden His face from you." Indeed, it is expressly written, that there is "no communion between light and darkness."[3] Now God is Light, and every sin is darkness in measure. So then, what greater stain could be cast upon God's wisdom, than to suggest He lacks a means whereby His children might perfectly serve and worship Him; or that He has not provided a way whereby they might cease to serve the devil? For "he that

---

3   2 Cor. 6:14

sins is the servant of sin,"[4] and every sin is an act of service and obedience to the devil. So then, if the saints must continue to sin daily, in thought, word and deed, and if their very service to God is mixed with sin (as our opposers insist), then surely they serve the devil as much or more than they serve the Lord!

Now, who would not be accounted a foolish master among men who, being willing and able to provide a way whereby his children and servants might serve him entirely, yet refused to do so, and instead allowed his servants to more fully and faithfully serve his avowed enemy? What then should we think of a doctrine that would infer this folly upon the omnipotent and only wise God?

Secondly, this doctrine is inconsistent with the justice of God. For since God requires purity from His children, and frequently commands them to abstain from every iniquity (as shall hereafter be seen); and since "His wrath is revealed against all ungodliness and unrighteousness of men,"[5] it must necessarily follow that He has given men the capacity to answer His will, or else He requires more than He has given power to perform. This, indeed, would be to openly declare Him unjust, and to say with the slothful servant, "You are a hard master!" We have previously spoken of the injustice that our opposers ascribe to God, in alleging that He damns the wicked without ever having afforded them the means of being saved. But this is a charge even more irrational and inconsistent—to suggest that God will not afford His own elect (whom they confess He loves) the means to please Him.

---

4   John 8:34; Romans 6:16
5   Romans 1:18

What can follow from so strange a doctrine? This imperfection in the saints either proceeds from God, or it is from themselves. If it proceeds from them, it must be because they fall short in making use of the power given to them—the grace whereby they are made capable to obey. But if it is not of themselves, then the imperfection must be of God, who has not seen fit to grant sufficient grace to answer His own requirement. And again, what is this but to attribute to God the height of injustice, to make Him require His children to forsake sin even while withholding the means to do so! Surely this makes God more unrighteous than the wicked men of whom Christ spoke in His sermon on the mount; for even they, when "their children ask for bread, will not give them a stone, or when they ask for fish, will not give them a serpent."[6] And though our adversaries confess that all ought to seek God for power to redeem from sin, yet they believe and teach that none should ever expect to receive such power. Is this not to make God as unjust to His children as Pharaoh was to the Israelites, in requiring brick and not giving them straw? But blessed be God, He does not so deal with those that truly trust in Him and wait upon Him, as these men vainly imagine. For the faithful ones indeed find His grace to be sufficient for them, and they know how to overcome the evil one by the gift of His power and Spirit.

Thirdly, this evil doctrine is highly injurious to Jesus Christ and greatly derogates from the power and virtue of His sacrifice, rendering His coming and ministry ineffectual. For one of the principal reasons for Christ's coming in the flesh was the removal of sin, and the gathering of a

---

[6] Matthew 7:9-11

righteous generation to serve the Lord in purity of mind, and to walk before Him in fear. It is He who "brought in everlasting righteousness,"[7] and that gospel perfection which the Law could not effect.[8] Hence He is said to have "given Himself for us, that He might redeem us from every lawless deed and purify for Himself His own special people, zealous for good works."[9] These words of the apostle are certainly spoken with regard to the saints while still upon earth. But contrary to this, our opponents affirm that we are never truly redeemed from all iniquity, and so they make Christ's "giving of Himself for us" void and ineffectual, denying that He really "purifies for himself a special people." But, I ask, how can a people be zealous for good works when they are daily committing evil ones? And how are they a purified people who still live in impurity, and sin continually? It is expressly written that, "For this purpose the Son of God was manifested, that He might destroy the works of the devil,"[10] and, "You know that He was manifested to take away our sins."[11] But these men make this purpose of no effect, for they will not believe that the Son of God destroys the works of the devil in this world, nor that Christ was manifest to take away our sins, seeing they plead a necessity of always living in them. And lest any should twist this Scripture as if it were spoken only of removing the *guilt* of sin, the apostle (as though seeking purposely to avoid such an objection) immediately adds,

---

7   Daniel 9:24
8   See Colossians 1:28; Hebrews 7:19, 9:9, 10:1
9   Titus 2:14
10   1 John 3:8
11   1 John 3:5

"Whosoever abides in Him does not sin;" and "Let no one deceive you. He who practices righteousness is righteous, just as He is righteous. He who sins is of the devil."[12]

Now, if Christ was manifest to take away sin, how strangely do these men overturn the doctrine of Christ by denying that sin is ever taken away here? Oh consider how injurious this is to the efficacy and power of Christ's appearance? Did not Christ come to gather a people out of sin into righteousness, out from the kingdom of Satan into the kingdom of the dear Son of God? And do not they who are gathered by Him become His servants, His children, His brethren, and His friends? Indeed, it is said of them "as He was, so are they in this world"[13]—holy, pure, and undefiled. And does not Christ still watch over them, stand by them, pray for them, preserve them by His Power and Spirit, walk in them and dwell among them, even as the devil, on the other hand, does among the reprobate ones? Why would the servants of Christ be less able to serve their Master than the servants of the devil serve theirs? Or is Christ unwilling to have His servants thoroughly pure (a gross blasphemy, contrary to many scriptures)? Or is Christ not able by His power to preserve and enable His children to serve Him (which is no less blasphemous to affirm)? But certainly, if the saints sin daily in thought, word, and deed, as these men assert, then they serve the devil daily, and continue subject to his power, and so he prevails more in them than Christ, and keeps them in bondage even contrary to Christ's will. But how greatly does this contradict the end of Christ's coming as it is

---

[12]   1 John 3:6-8

[13]   1 John 4:17

expressed by the apostle: "Even as Christ also loved the church and gave Himself for her, that He might sanctify and cleanse her with the washing of water by the word, that He might present her to Himself a glorious church, not having spot or wrinkle or any such thing, but that she should be holy and without blemish."[14] Now, if Christ has really accomplished the thing for which He came, then the members of His body are not always to be sinning in thought, word, and deed. Otherwise, there is no difference between being sanctified and unsanctified, clean and unclean, holy and unholy, being daily blemished with sin, and being without blemish.

Fourthly, this doctrine renders the work of the ministry, the preaching of the Word, the writing of the Scriptures, and the prayers of holy men altogether useless and ineffectual. As to the first (Eph. 4:11-13), pastors and teachers are said to be "given for the perfection of the saints," etc., "till we all come in the unity of the faith and of the knowledge of the Son of God, unto a perfect man, unto the measure of the stature of the fullness of Christ." Now, if there is a necessity of sinning daily, and in all things, then there can be no perfection. Moreover, these ministers, who assure us that we need never expect to be delivered from sin, do they not render their own work needless? For what need is there for preaching against sin, if sin can never be forsaken? And with regard to the Scriptures, our adversaries highly exalt them in their words, often extolling their usefulness and perfection. Indeed, the apostle tells us (2 Tim. 3:17) that the "Scriptures are profitable for doctrine, for reproof, for correction, for instruction in righteousness,

---

[14] Ephesians 5:25-27

that the man of God may be perfect, thoroughly furnished unto all good works." But if it be denied that this is attainable in this life, then the Scriptures are to no profit, for what use shall we have of them in the next life? Furthermore, this doctrine renders the prayers of the saints altogether useless; for why should we pray daily that God deliver us from evil and free us from sin by the help of His Spirit and Grace (as all confess we ought) if such a thing be unattainable in this life? Yet the holy apostles prayed earnestly for this end, and therefore (no doubt) believed it attainable here. For they were "always laboring fervently for them in prayers, that they may stand perfect and complete in all the will of God."[15] They prayed that God would "establish their hearts blameless in holiness,"[16] and "sanctify them entirely, spirit, soul, and body,"[17] etc.

But fifthly, this doctrine is contrary to common sense and reason. For sin and righteousness are as two opposite seeds—the one ruling in the children of darkness, the other in the children of Light. And as men are respectively leavened and governed by them, so they are accounted either reprobated or justified, seeing it is an "abomination in the sight of God either to justify the wicked or to condemn the just."[18] Now to say that men cannot be so leavened with the one as to become delivered from the other, is, in plain words, to affirm that sin and righteousness are compatible, and that a man may be truly termed righteous, though he be daily sinning in everything he does. And then what dif-

---

[15] Colossians 4:12
[16] 1 Thessalonians 3:13
[17] 1 Thessalonians 5:23
[18] Proverbs 17:15

ference is there between good and evil? Is this not to fall into that great abomination of "putting light for darkness," and "calling good evil, and evil good?"[19] For they say the very best actions of God's children are defiled and polluted, and that those who sin daily in thought, word, and deed are good men and women, even the saints and holy servants of the holy and pure God. Can there be anything more repugnant to common reason than this? Where are the purified ones of whom the Scriptures speak? Where are they who were formerly unholy, but now have been washed and made holy;[20] who were formerly darkness, but now are light in the Lord?[21] According to this sinful doctrine there can indeed be none.

Evidence from Scripture

For the further demonstration of the truth, I shall now proceed to the second thing proposed by me, namely, to prove our position from several testimonies of the holy Scriptures.

First, I prove it from the absolute, positive command of Christ and His apostles to keep the commandments, and to be perfect in this respect, knowing that God requires no impossible thing. Now, that this is plainly commanded in the New Testament, without any commentary or consequence, is evident in the following Scripture testimonies: Matthew 5:48, "Therefore you shall be perfect, just as your Father in heaven is perfect." 1 Corinthians 7:19, "Circumci-

---

[19]   Isaiah 5:20
[20]   1 Corinthians 6:11
[21]   Ephesians 5:8

sion is nothing, and uncircumcision is nothing, but the keeping of the commandments of God." 1 John 2:3-6, "Now by this we know that we know Him, if we keep His commandments. He who says, 'I know Him,' and does not keep His commandments, is a liar, and the truth is not in him. But whoever keeps His word, truly the love of God is perfected in him. By this we know that we are in Him." 1 John 3:5-10, "And you know that He was manifested to take away our sins, and in Him there is no sin. Whoever abides in Him does not sin. Whoever sins has neither seen Him nor known Him. Little children, let no one deceive you. He who practices righteousness is righteous, just as He is righteous. He who sins is of the devil, for the devil has sinned from the beginning. For this purpose the Son of God was manifested, that He might destroy the works of the devil. Whoever has been born of God does not sin, for His seed remains in him; and he cannot sin, because he has been born of God. In this the children of God and the children of the devil are manifest: Whoever does not practice righteousness is not of God, nor is he who does not love his brother." See also Matt. 7:21, John 13:17; 1 Cor. 7:19; 2 Cor. 13:11. All of these scriptures intimate a positive command for the keeping of His commandments, and declare the absolute necessity of it. Therefore, as if they had been purposely written to answer the objections of our opposers, they show the folly of those that will esteem themselves children or friends of God, while they do otherwise.

Secondly, such a freedom from sin is possible because we receive the Gospel for that very purpose. This is expressly promised to us as we come under the dominion of grace, as appears by these scriptures: Romans 6:14, "For sin shall not have dominion over you, for you are not under Law but under Grace." Romans 8:3-4, "For what the Law could not do in that it was weak through the flesh, God did by sending His own Son... that the righteous requirement of the law might be fulfilled in us," etc. For if this were not a condition both necessary and attainable under the Gospel, there would be no difference between "the Law, which made nothing perfect," and "the bringing in of a better hope,"[22] nor between those who are under the Gospel and mere legalists. But the apostle, throughout the whole sixth chapter to the Romans argues not only the possibility, but the necessity of being free from sin by coming under the Gospel and under Grace, and being no longer under the Law. In verses 2-7 he states this to be the condition of himself and those to whom he writes, and then in 11-13 and 16-18 he argues both the possibility and the necessity of freedom from sin, saying "Therefore do not let sin reign in your mortal body, that you should obey it in its lusts," and, "Having been set free from sin, you became slaves of righteousness." Finally, in the 22nd verse, he declares his readers in measure to have attained this condition, in these words, "But now having been set free from sin, and having become slaves of God, you have your fruit to holiness, and the end, everlasting life."

Now, even as this perfection or freedom from sin is attained and made possible where the Gospel and inward law of the Spirit is received and known, so the ignorance of this inward life and power has been and is the reason why so many oppose this truth. For man, not minding the Light

---

[22]   Hebrews 7:19

or Law within his heart, which not only discovers sin but leads out of it, remains a stranger to the new Life and Birth that is born of God, which naturally does His will, and cannot, of its own nature, transgress His commandments. Such a man, in his natural state, looks at the commandments of God as they are without him, in the letter, and finds himself reproved and convicted, and by the letter killed but not made alive. And so, finding himself wounded, and not applying himself inwardly to that Light and Grace which can heal, he labors in his own will after a conformity to the Law as it is written in words, which he can never obtain, but finds that the more he wrestles, the more he falls short. Though these may have a notion of Christianity, and an external faith in Christ, still they are, in effect, in the state of the Jew, with his carnal commandment, his external law, in the first covenant state which "makes not the comers thereunto perfect as pertaining to the conscience" (Heb. 9:9). This has made them strain and twist the Scriptures for an imputed righteousness wholly from without, in order to cover their ongoing impurities, and to imagine an acceptance with God to be possible, even while they hold it impossible ever to obey Christ's commands.

But alas, O deceived souls! This will not avail in the Day wherein God will judge "every man according to what he has done, whether good or bad."[23] It will not save you to say it was necessary to sin daily in thought, word, and deed; for those who do so have most certainly "obeyed unrighteousness."[24] And what is the end of these but tribu-

---

[23]   2 Corinthians 5:10
[24]   Romans 2:8

lation and anguish, indignation and wrath; even as glory, honor, peace, and immortality are promised to such as have done good and patiently continued in well-doing. So then, if you desire to know this perfection and freedom from sin made possible for you, turn your mind to the Light and spiritual Law of Christ in the heart, and submit to its reproofs. Bear the judgment and indignation of God upon the unrighteous nature in you according as it is revealed, which Christ has made tolerable for you; and so suffer "judgment" in you to be "brought forth into victory."[25] In this way you will come to partake of the fellowship of Christ's sufferings and be made conformable unto His death.[26] You will feel yourself crucified with Him to the world by the power of His cross in you, so that that life which formerly was alive in you to this world, and to its love and lust, may die, and a new life be raised by which you may live from now on unto God and not to or for yourself. Then you will truly be able to say with the apostle, "I have been crucified with Christ; it is no longer I who live, but Christ lives in me."[27] Then you will be a Christian indeed, and not one in name only, as too many are. Then you will know what it is to have "put off the old man with his deeds," who indeed sins daily in thought, word, and deed; and to have "put on the new man, that is renewed in

---

[25] Matthew 12:20. Editor's Note: Many modern translations use the word *justice* in place of *judgment,* but the Greek word is indeed judgment (*krisis*). The same is true of the Hebrew word in Isaiah 42 from which this quotation in Matthew is taken *(mishpat,* i.e. judgment).

[26] Philippians 3:10

[27] Galatians 2:20

holiness, after the image of Him that has created him."[28] And you will witness yourself to be "God's workmanship created in Christ Jesus unto good works."[29] And to this new man "Christ's yoke is easy, and His burden is light;"[30] though it is heavy to the old Adam. Yes, the commandments of God are not grievous unto this new man; for it is his food and drink to be found fulfilling the will of God.

Objections Considered

But I shall proceed now to answer the objections and arguments of our opposers.

Objection: I shall begin with their chief and great argument, which is the words of the apostle John: "If we say that we have no sin, we deceive ourselves, and the Truth is not in us."[31] This they think invincible.

Answer: But this objection does not suit their purpose, for John does not say we sin daily in thought, word, and deed, far less that the very good works which God works in us by His Spirit are sin. Indeed, the very next verse clearly shows that upon confession and repentance we are not only forgiven but also cleansed: "He is faithful to forgive us our sins, and to cleanse us from all unrighteousness." Here is both a forgiveness and removing of the guilt, and a cleansing or removing of the filth; for it would be both senseless

---

[28] Ephesians 4:24
[29] Ephesians 2:10
[30] Matthew 11:30
[31] 1 John 1:8

and repetitive to make both forgiveness and cleansing belong to the removing of guilt. For this reason, having known both the guilt and the filth of sin removed, the apostle continues in the past tense in verse 10 saying, "If we say we have not *sinned*, we make Him a liar."

Furthermore, as Augustine well observed in his exposition upon the epistle to the Galatians, "It is one thing not to sin, and another thing not to have sin." The apostle's words are not, "If we say we do not commit not sin daily, we deceive ourselves;" but "if we say we have no sin." And between these two statements there is a great difference! For we freely acknowledge that all have sinned, and that all may be said in this sense to have sin. Moreover, "sin" may be taken for the seed of sin which is in all men, even in those who are redeemed from actual sinning. But as to the temptations and provocations that proceed from this seed, when resisted by grace in the servants of God and not yielded to, the sin belongs to the devil who tempts, and not to the man who is preserved.

But the whole of this controversy is necessary, for the very same apostle, in several places of the same epistle, plainly and positively asserts the possibility of freedom from sin, as has been mentioned already.

Objection: Their second objection is from two places of Scripture, which say very much the same thing. The one is 1 Kings 8:46, "For there is no man that does not sin." The other is Ecclesiastes 7:20, "For there is not a just man upon earth, that does good, and does not sin."

Answer: I answer, first, that these verses speak nothing of a daily and continual sinning, so as never to be redeemed from it, but only that all have sinned, or that there is none that does not sin. Secondly, there is something to be said for the covenant and dispensation in which these were written; for even if it should be granted that in Solomon's time there was none who did not sin, it will not necessarily follow that there are none such now, or that it is not now attainable by the grace of God under the Gospel. And lastly, this whole objection hangs upon a false interpretation of Scripture; for the Hebrew word *yekhta'* may be read in the potential mood, thus rendering it "There is no man who *may not* sin," which indeed is how it is translated from the Hebrew by Junius and Tremellius, and also Vatablus. The same word is similarly translated in the potential mood in Psalm 119:11, "I have hidden Your word in my heart, that I *may not* sin against You." And seeing that this translation is more congruent with the universal scope of the Scriptures, the testimony of the Truth, and the sense of almost all interpreters, it doubtless ought to be so understood.

Objection: Thirdly, they object from some expressions of the apostle Paul in Romans chapter 7: "For the good that I will to do, I do not do; but the evil I will not to do, that I practice."[32] And "O wretched man that I am! Who shall deliver me from the body of this death?"[33]

Answer: I answer, there is nothing in the text which would suggest him to be speaking of his present condition, or of a

---

[32]   Romans 7:19
[33]   Romans 7:24

condition that he must always be under. On the contrary, in the former chapter (as has been mentioned at large), he insists that Christians, being "dead to sin," should no longer live therein. It is apparent then, that the apostle here speaks of a condition he had formerly known, or that he impersonates (for the benefit of his readers) the condition of one not yet come to maturity, which is common in Scripture.

Now, that Paul does not here speak of his present condition is evident, for previously in this chapter he says (vs. 5), "For when we *were* in the flesh, the sinful passions which were aroused by the law were at work in our members to bear fruit to death;" and (vs. 9) "I *was alive once* without the law, but when the commandment came, sin revived and I died." And later he says (vs. 14), "We know that the law is spiritual, but I am carnal, sold under sin." But are we to imagine that the apostle Paul was a carnal man at the time of writing this epistle? Does he not plainly inform us how he was not left in this condition, but indeed witnessed deliverance from it? For after his exclamation, "Who will set me free from the body of this death," he happily answers his own question, saying, "I thank God— through Jesus Christ our Lord,"[34] and then affirms that "the law of the Spirit of Life in Christ Jesus" had "made him free from the law of sin and death," so that "the righteous requirement of the law might be fulfilled in us who do not walk according to the flesh but according to the Spirit."[35]

---

[34] Romans 7:25
[35] Romans 8:2-4

Objection: Fourthly, they object from the faults and sins of several eminent saints, such as Noah, David, etc.

Answer: I answer, this does not at all prove our opponent's case; for the question is not whether good men may not fall into sin (which we do not deny), but whether it is impossible for them not to sin. Nor does it follow that, because these men sinned on certain occasions, that they always sinned, and so never experienced times of true freedom from sin.

Objection: Lastly, they object from the prayer of our Lord, where He taught His disciples to say, "forgive us our trespasses, as we forgive those who trespass against us."[36]

Answer: I answer, we deny not that "all have sinned, and fall short of the glory of God,"[37] and that all therefore need to pray that their past sins may be blotted out, and that they may be daily preserved from sinning. But if some dare say that hoping or believing to be made free from sin hinders praying for forgiveness of sin, it would follow by the same rule that "we should continue in sin so that grace may abound;"[38] for the more men commit sin, the more plentiful occasion there would be of asking forgiveness of sin. But the apostle has sufficiently refuted such sin-pleasing babblings in his response to this very controversy, saying, "May it never be! How shall we who died to sin live any longer in it?"[39]

---

[36] Matthew 6:12

[37] Romans 3:23

[38] Romans 6:1

[39] Romans 6:2

To conclude then—blessed are they that believe in Him, who is both able and willing to deliver from all sin, as many as come to Him through true repentance, and who do not resolve (as our adversaries do) to be the devil's servants all their lifetime, but daily go on forsaking unrighteousness, forgetting those things that are behind, and "pressing forward toward the mark, for the prize of the high calling of God, in Christ Jesus."[40] Such as these shall find their faith and confidence not to be in vain, and in due time shall be made conquerors through Him in whom they have believed; and so, overcoming, they shall be established as "pillars in the house of God," so as "to go out no more."[41]

---

[40] Philippians 3:14
[41] Revelation 3:12

Made in the USA
Middletown, DE
08 February 2017